BRIGHT & Brainy

3rd Grade Practice

Author

Suzanne Barchers, Ed.D

SHELL EDUCATION

Publishing Credits

Dona Herweck Rice, *Editor-in-Chief*; Robin Erickson, *Production Director*;
Lee Aucoin, *Creative Director;* Timothy J. Bradley, *Illustration Manager*;
Sara Johnson, M.S.Ed, *Senior Editor*; Evelyn Garcia, *Associate Education Editor;*
Leah Quillian, *Assistant Editor;* Grace Alba, *Designer*;
Corinne Burton, M.A.Ed., *Publisher*

Standard

© 2010 National Governors Association Center for Best Practices and Council of Chief State School Officers (CCSS)

Shell Education
5301 Oceanus Drive
Huntington Beach, CA 92649-1030
http://www.shelleducation.com
ISBN 978-1-4258-0886-0
© 2012 Shell Educational Publishing, Inc.
Reprinted 2013

Table of Contents

Every Child Is Bright and Brainy

The Need for Continual Practice

"Practice makes perfect."

That's what they say, and it's usually true! Although educational practices have changed over time, some key methods have stayed the same. Children need plenty of opportunity to practice skills and show what they know. The more they do, the more they can transfer their learning to everyday life—and future success!

Of course, there has to be a good purpose for the practice. That is where the pages in this book come in. Created with the essential standards in mind, each activity page focuses on a particular concept, skill, or skill-set and provides students abundant opportunities to practice and achieve mastery.

Annis and Annis (1987) found that continual repetition helps increase the levels of the Bloom cognitive domain. In other words, practice helps students learn in a wide variety of ways at all levels of cognitive ability. It provides students opportunities to think more deeply about the subjects they are studying. Marzano (2010) asserts that in order for students to independently display their learning, it is necessary for them to practice procedural skills. Providing students with ample opportunity to practice remains a key strategy for employing the best educational practices in or out of the classroom.

Every Child Is Bright and Brainy *(cont.)*

Understanding the Standards

The Common Core State Standards were developed in collaboration with a wide variety of educators through the Common Core State Standards Initiative. The goal was to create a clear and consistent framework to prepare students for higher education and the workforce. To this end, teachers, school administrators, and other educational experts worked together in a state-led effort coordinated by the National Governors Association Center for Best Practices (NGA) and the Council of Chief State School Officers (CCSSO).

The standards incorporate the most effective models from around the country and around the globe, providing teachers and parents with a shared understanding of what students are expected to learn. The consistency of the standards provides a common, appropriate benchmark for students unrelated to their location.

According to the NGA and the CCSSO, these standards meet the following criteria:

- ☼ They are aligned with college and work expectations;

- ☼ They are clear, understandable, and consistent;

- ☼ They include rigorous content and application of knowledge through high-order skills;

- ☼ They build upon strengths and lessons of current state standards;

- ☼ They are informed by other top-performing countries so that all students are prepared to succeed in our global economy and society; and

- ☼ They are evidence-based

Students who meet these standards within their K–12 education should have the skills and knowledge necessary to succeed in their educational careers and beyond.

Making It Work

It is important for you to understand the key features of this book, so that you can use it in a way that works for you and your students.

- **Standards-based practice.** The exercises in *Bright & Brainy: 3rd Grade Practice* are aligned with the Common Core State Standards. Each activity page focuses on a particular concept, skill, or skill-set and provides students ample opportunities to practice and achieve mastery.

- **Clear, easy-to-understand activities.** The exercises in this book are written in a kid-friendly style.

- **Assessment of student progress.** Based on student progress, the Common Core State Standards Correlation Chart (pages 9–10) helps identify the grade-level standards with which students may need additional support.

- **Reinforcement of key grade-level concepts.** Each activity provides practice of key grade-level language arts and mathematics skills in an organized and meaningful way.

- **Stand-alone activity pages.** Each activity is flexible and can be used independently in a variety of instructional or at-home settings.

The chart below provides suggestions for how to implement the activities.

Whole/Small Group	Individual	At Home/Homework
• Read and discuss the directions at the beginning of each activity. Work practice problems on an interactive whiteboard, document camera, or other display method. • Have students work problems on the interactive whiteboard. • Have students take turns reading each question. • Display the problems and review and correct them. • Read and discuss responses.	• Create folders for each student. Include a copy of their selected activity pages. • Collect work and check student answers, or provide each student with copies of the answer key and allow them to check their own work. • Select specific activity pages to support individual students' needs for additional practice.	• Provide each student with activity pages to reinforce skills. • Collect work and check student answers, or provide each student with copies of the answer key and allow them to check their own work. • Select specific activity pages to provide extra support in areas where individual students may need additional practice.

Making It Work (cont.)

Bright & Brainy: 3rd Grade Practice provides practice pages for a broad range of Common Core language arts and mathematics standards. Language arts topics are designed to provide students practice in the most vital skills included in the Common Core Standards. These range from reading foundational skills to fluency, and from writing to speaking and listening. Activities designed to support student learning of how to read informational texts, literature, and vocabulary skills round out the carefully chosen exercises. Within each of these broad areas are individual activity pages centering on subtopics, such as letter recognition, alike and different, antonyms, and rhyming. Each covered skill is crucial to achieving language fluency and to setting the stage for future success in language arts. Likewise, the chosen mathematics skills represent fundamental and integral topics from the Common Core Standards. Clear, student-friendly exercises center around the essential areas of counting and cardinal numbers, number and operations in base ten, operations and algebraic thinking, measuring, data, and geometry.

Individual lessons engage students in mastering specific skills, including more, less, same, sequencing, alike and different, and flat vs. solid.

This book covers the following:

- Reading: Foundational Skills
- Language Conventions
- Reading: Informational Text
- Vocabulary Acquisition and Use
- Reading: Literature
- Fluency
- Writing

- Speaking and Listening
- Number and Operations in Base Ten
- Operations and Algebraic Thinking
- Number and Operations—Fractions
- Measurement and Data
- Geometry

Additionally, the Resource CD allows for easy access to the student activity pages in this book. Electronic PDF files of all the activity pages are included on the CD.

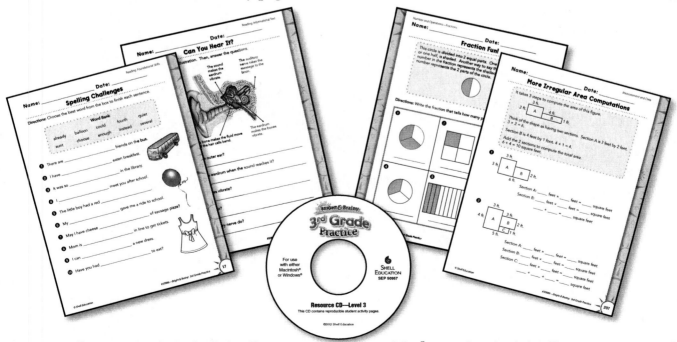

Language Arts Activity Pages   **Mathematics Activity Pages**

Correlation to Standards

Shell Education is committed to producing educational materials that are research and standards based. In this effort, we have correlated all of our products to the academic standards of all 50 United States, the District of Columbia, the Department of Defense Dependent Schools, and all Canadian provinces. We have also correlated to the Common Core State Standards.

How to Find Standards Correlations

To print a customized correlation report of this product for your state, visit our website at **http://www.shelleducation.com** and follow the on-screen directions. If you require assistance in printing correlation reports, please contact Customer Service at 1-800-858-7339.

Purpose and Intent of Standards

Legislation mandates that all states adopt academic standards that identify the skills students will learn in kindergarten through grade twelve. Many states also have standards for Pre-K. This same legislation sets requirements to ensure the standards are detailed and comprehensive.

Standards are designed to focus instruction and guide adoption of curricula. Standards are statements that describe the criteria necessary for students to meet specific academic goals. They define the knowledge, skills, and content students should acquire at each level. Standards are also used to develop standardized tests to evaluate students' academic progress.

Teachers are required to demonstrate how their lessons meet state standards. State standards are used in development of all of our products, so educators can be assured they meet the academic requirements of each state.

Common Core State Standards

The lessons in this book are aligned to the Common Core State Standards (CCSS). The standards listed on pages 9–10 support the objectives presented throughout the lessons.

Common Core State Standards Correlation Chart

Language Arts	
Reading: Foundational Skills	**Page(s)**
RF.3.3—Identify and know the meaning of the most common prefixes and derivational suffixes	11–14
RF.3.3—Decode words with common Latin suffixes	13–14
RF.3.3—Decode multisyllable words	15–16
RF.3.3—Read grade-appropriate irregularly spelled words	17–18
Language Conventions	**Page(s)**
L.3.1—Explain the function of nouns, pronouns, verbs, adjectives, and adverbs in general and their functions in particular sentences	19–28
L.3.1—Form and use regular and irregular plural nouns	29–32
L.3.1—Use abstract nouns	33–34
L.3.1—Form and use regular and irregular verbs	35–36
L.3.1—Form and use simple verb tenses	37–38
L.3.1—Ensure subject-verb and pronoun-antecedent agreement	39–40
L.3.1—Use coordinating and subordinating conjunctions	41–42
L.3.1—Produce simple, compound, and complex sentences	43–46
L.3.2—Capitalize appropriate words in titles	47–48
L.3.2—Use commas in addresses	49
L.3.2—Use commas and quotation marks in dialogue	50–51
L.3.2—Form and use possessives	52–53
L.3.2—Use spelling patterns and generalizations in writing words	54–58
L.3.2—Use syllable patterns in writing words	58–61
L.3.3—Choose words and phrases for effect	62–64
L.3.3—Recognize and observe differences between the conventions of spoken and written standard English	65–66
Reading: Informational Text	**Page(s)**
RI.3.1—Ask and answer questions to demonstrate understanding of a text	67–82
RI.3.2—Determine the main idea of a text; recount the key details and explain how they support the main idea	67–82
RI.3.4—Determine the meaning of general academic and domain-specific words and phrases in a text	83–86
RI.3.5—Use text features and search tools to locate information relevant to a given topic efficiently	87–90
RI.3.6—Distinguish their own point of view from that of the author of a text	91–94
RI.3.7—Use information gained from illustrations and the words in a text to demonstrate understanding of the text	95–96
RI.3.8—Describe the logical connection between particular sentences and paragraphs in a text	97–102
Vocabulary Acquisition and Use	**Page(s)**
L.3.4—Determine the meaning of the new word formed when a known affix is added to a known word	103–104
L. 3.4—Use a known root word as a clue to the meaning of an unknown word with the same root	105–106
L.3.4—Use glossaries or beginning dictionaries, both print and digital, to determine or clarify meaning of key words	107–108
L.3.5—Distinguish the literal and nonliteral meanings of words and phrases in context	109–110
L.3.5—Identify real-life connections between words and their use	111–112
L.3.5—Distinguish shades of meanings among related words that describe states of mind or degrees of certainty	113–115
L.3.6—Acquire and use accurately grade-appropriate conversational, general academic, and domain-specific words and phrases	116

Common Core State Standards Correlation Chart (cont.)

Language Arts (cont.)	
Literature	**Page(s)**
RL.3.1—Ask and answer questions to demonstrate understanding of a text	117–120
RL.3.2.—Recount stories, including fables, folktales, and myths from diverse cultures	121–124
RL. 3.4—Determine the meaning of words and phrases as they are used in a text	125–126
RL.3.5—Refer to parts of stories, dramas, and poems when writing or speaking about a text	127
RL.3.7—Explain how specific aspects of a text's illustrations contribute to what is conveyed by the words in a story	128
RL.3.9—Compare and contrast the themes, settings, and plots of stories	129–130
Fluency	**Page(s)**
RF.3.4—Read with sufficient accuracy and fluency to support comprehension	131–132
Writing	**Page(s)**
W.3.1–8—Write opinion pieces on topics or texts, supporting a point of view with reasons	133–140
Speaking and Listening	**Page(s)**
SL.3.1–3.5—Engage effectively in a range of collaborative dicussions with diverse partners	141, 143
Mathematics	
Number and Operations in Base Ten	**Page(s)**
3.NBT.1—Use place value understanding to round whole numbers to the nearest 10 or 100	144–147
3.NBT.2—Fluently add and subtract within 1,000 using strategies and algorithms	148–153
3.NBT.3—Multiply one-digit whole numbers by multiples of 10 in the range 10–90	154–156
Operations and Algebraic Thinking	**Page(s)**
3.OA.1—Interpret products of whole numbers	157–158
3.OA.3—Use multiplication and division within 100 to solve word problems	159
3.OA.4—Determine the unknown whole number in a multiplication or division equation	160–163
3.OA.7—Fluently multiply and divide within 100	164–166
3.OA.8—Solve two-step problems using the four operations	167–173
3.OA.9—Identify arithmetic patterns, and explain them using properties of operations	174–175
Number and Operations—Fractions	**Page(s)**
3.NF.1—Understand a fraction $1/b$ as the quantity formed by 1 part when a whole is partitioned into b equal parts	176–177
3.NF.2—Understand a fraction as a number on the number line	178–182
3.NF.3—Explain equivalence of fractions in special cases, and compare fractions by reasoning about their size	183–188
Measurement and Data	**Page(s)**
3.MD.1—Tell and write time to the nearest minute and measure time intervals in minutes	189–190
3.MD.2—Measure and estimate liquid volumes and masses of objects using standard units of grams	191–192
3.MD.3—Draw a scaled picture graph and a scaled bar graph to represent a data set with several categories	193–195
3.MD.4—Generate measurement data by measuring lengths using rulers marked with halves and fourths of an inch	196–197
3.MD.6—Measure areas by counting unit squares	198–199
3.MD.7—Relate area to the operations of multiplication and addition	200–207
3.MD.8—Solve real world and mathematical problems involving perimeters	208–210
Geometry	**Page(s)**
3.G.1—Understand that shapes in different categories may share attributes, and that the shared attributes can define a larger category	211–213
3.G.2—Partition shapes into parts with equal areas	213–214

Name: _____ **Date:** _____

Prefix Challenge

A **prefix** is a word part added to the beginning of a word. It changes the meaning of the word.

Directions: Read each sentence. Choose the correct word.

Word Bank

misbehaved   impolite   mistreat   impure   impatient

1 Do not _____ your toys.

2 You should not be rude or _____ to your teacher.

3 The water from the lake is _____. Don't drink it.

4 My friend got in trouble. He _____ in class.

5 Bert was _____ for the movie to start.

Name: _____ **Date:** _____

Suffix Challenges

A **suffix** is a word part added to the end of a word. It changes the meaning of the word.

Directions: Read each sentence. Choose the correct word.

Word Bank

builder   tricky   itchy   frosty   painter

1 I got a mosquito bite. It is _____.

2 He loves making things with tools. He is a _____.

3 Her artwork is beautiful. She has been a _____ for years.

4 It is so cold that the window is

_____.

5 The game is difficult to win. It is really

_____.

Name: _____ **Date:** _____

More Suffix Challenges

A **suffix** is a word part added to the end of a word. It changes the meaning of the word.

Directions: Read each sentence. Choose the correct word.

Word Bank

direction   operation   addition   usable   believable

1 The doctor did a careful _____.

2 I think I am lost. I do not know which _____ to go.

3 Do you think that big shelf is _____?

4 His story is very _____.

5 Use _____ to solve the problem.

Name: _____ **Date:** _____

Prefix and Suffix Round Up

Directions: Draw a line to connect the word with the correct meaning.

1 unfair   make firm

2 rewash   wrong

3 washable   something that can be laundered

4 bendable   make limp

5 likeable   honest

6 unbend   something that can be twisted

7 dislike   make something clean again

8 harden   straighten

9 truthful   hate

10 soften   something that can be enjoyed

Name: _____ Date: _____

Decode Multisyllabic Words

A **syllable** is a unit that can be pronounced. It has one vowel.
Long words can be divided into syllables.

Directions: Divide the words into syllables.

1 attic _____

2 cannot _____

3 common _____

4 cottage _____

5 cotton _____

6 dollar _____

7 fatten _____

8 fossil _____

9 gallon _____

10 gossip _____

Name: _____ **Date:** _____

Decode More Multisyllabic Words

A **syllable** is a unit that can be pronounced. It has one vowel. Long words can be divided into syllables.

Directions: Divide the words into syllables.

1 cactus _____

2 content _____

3 dentist _____

4 forgot _____

5 helmet _____

6 hundred _____

7 husband _____

8 master _____

9 mental _____

10 mistake _____

Name: _____ **Date:** _____

Spelling Challenges

Directions: Choose the best word from the box to finish each sentence.

Word Bank

already	balloon	could	fourth	quiet
aunt	choose	enough	instead	several

1 There are _____ friends on the bus.

2 I have _____ eaten breakfast.

3 It was so _____ in the library.

4 I _____ meet you after school.

5 The little boy had a red _____.

6 My _____ gave me a ride to school.

7 May I have cheese _____ of sausage pizza?

8 Mom is _____ in line to get tickets.

9 I can _____ a new dress.

10 Have you had _____ to eat?

Name: _____ **Date:** _____

More Spelling Challenges

Directions: Choose the best word from the box to finish each sentence.

Word Bank

along	children	cupboard	quite	together
among	country	early	sugar	weather

1 Do not worry. We are _____ friends.

2 Get the cereal from the _____.

3 We got to school very _____.

4 Are you and Denny going home _____?

5 That soda has too much _____ in it.

6 Those _____ want to get on the bus.

7 What will the _____ be tomorrow? Sunny or rainy?

8 She is _____ happy with her game.

9 I walked _____ the edge of the lake.

10 The farm is out in the _____.

Language Conventions

Name: _____ **Date:** _____

Name That Noun!

A **noun** is a word for a person, place, thing, or idea. Words like *child, city, key,* and *joy* are nouns.

Directions: Circle the nouns. *Hint:* There are at least two nouns in each sentence.

1 Mary Jane rode the horse in a race.

2 We had chores to do after the race.

3 Mary Jane brushed the horse.

4 Dad left to get gas in the car.

5 Josh chopped up firewood to make a fire.

6 Max finished folding the clothes.

7 I put my clothes in the drawers.

8 Mom got matches for the fire.

9 We roasted hot dogs and marshmallows.

10 We watched the moon and stars come out.

© Shell Education

#50886—Bright & Brainy: 3rd Grade Practice

19

Name: _____ Date: _____

Noun Search

> A **noun** is a word for a person, place, thing, or idea. Words like *Jack, field, flower,* and *wish* are nouns.

Directions: Circle the nouns. *Hint:* There are at least two nouns in each sentence.

1 Our family went to an island for our vacation.

2 We took a ferry across the lake.

3 Dad drove our car onto the ferry.

4 We slept in a cabin on the boat that night.

5 The ferry is tied up at the dock.

6 Annie and I helped set up our tents near the beach.

7 Mom and I got lunch ready.

8 We got our swimsuits and rafts.

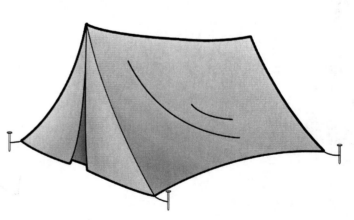

9 Annie and I jumped in the waves.

10 Mom and Dad floated on the rafts.

Name: _____ **Date:** _____

Acting Up!

> **Verbs** are action words. They tell what is happening in the sentence. *Climb* and *dance* are examples of verbs.

Directions: Write a sentence for each picture. Circle the verb in your sentence.

1 _____

_____

_____

2 _____

_____

_____

3 _____

_____

_____

4 _____

_____

_____

5 _____

_____

_____

Name: _____ **Date:** _____

All About Action

Verbs are action words. They tell what is happening in the sentence, such as *eating*.

Directions: Choose the best verb to complete each sentence.

Word Bank

| bit | chew | chomps | dine | gobbles |
| laps | munches | nibbles | slurp | snack |

❶ My grandmother likes to _____ in fancy restaurants.

❷ The dog _____ the food in the dish.

❸ The kitten _____ her milk.

❹ Mom says not to _____ your soup.

❺ It takes a long time to _____ taffy.

❻ The bear _____ up the meat.

❼ The horse _____ an apple.

❽ The mouse _____ a piece of cheese.

❾ My tooth fell out when I _____ down on the corn.

❿ My dentist said not to _____ between meals.

Name: _____ **Date:** _____

Noun or Verb?

Directions: Decide if the words are nouns or verbs. Write it in the correct box.

Word Bank

add	ant	April	arrive	sky
camera	decide	eagle	exclaim	forgive
holiday	imagine	joy	meal	notice
prepare	prove	ribbon	spider	behave

Nouns	Verbs

Name: _____ **Date:** _____

Amazing Adjectives

Adjectives are words that describe nouns. *Little, hot,* and *terrific* are adjectives. They can be used to describe nouns.

Directions: List adjectives below.

❶ List three adjectives that describe you.

_____

_____

❷ List three adjectives that describe your favorite dessert.

_____

_____

❸ List three adjectives that describe your favorite place to play.

_____

_____

Directions: Circle the adjective in each sentence.

❹ The scary dragon stomped through the forest.

❺ The dragon breathed fire through its huge nose.

❻ The brave knight rode his horse after the dragon.

❼ The dragon stopped suddenly. Its slimy scales glistened in the sun.

❽ The dragon turned. Its pale eyes narrowed as it saw the knight.

Name: _____ **Date:** _____

Adjective Fun

Adjectives can answer questions, such as *How many?*, *What kind?*, or *Which one?*

Directions: Finish the story by writing adjectives in the blanks.

Training My Parrot

I was so excited when I got my _____

parrot. First, I named him Perry. Then, I realized I had some

_____ work ahead. I wanted the parrot to

step onto my _____ finger. First I needed a

_____ command. I chose "Step up." Then, I

put my _____ finger out for Perry. I said, "Step

up." Do you know what that _____ parrot did? It

bit my finger! I knew that _____ parrots will do

that. So I said, "No," in a _____ voice. I moved

my finger closer. Perry pushed at my finger. I didn't move. Then,

that _____ parrot stepped right onto my finger!

I praised him, saying, "_____ Perry!"

Name: _____ **Date:** _____

Adverb Action

> **Adverbs** are words that describe a verb. They tell how, where, or when. They often end in *-ly*.

Directions: Finish each sentence by adding an adverb from the Word Bank. *Hint:* There can be more than one correct answer.

Word Bank

carefully	firmly	frantically	gladly	gradually	happily
instantly	quickly	slowly	softly	steadily	

1 I was _____ snorkeling in the ocean.

2 The fish swam _____ by me.

3 Suddenly the fish started swimming _____.

4 A huge shark glided _____ by me.

5 I knew I needed to swim _____.

6 But I couldn't help it. I started to swim _____ toward the boat.

7 The group leader _____ tapped me on the shoulder.

8 I _____ calmed down.

9 The shark _____ drifted away.

10 The fish started swimming _____ again.

Name: _____ **Date:** _____

Adverbs

> **Adverbs** can tell when or where something was done.

Directions: Circle the adverbs that describe when or where the event happened.

1 We went on a hayride yesterday.

2 The horses were outside.

3 The leader always sings songs on the ride.

4 He never lets us get bored.

5 The horses first went north.

6 I wish I could go again.

7 Next, we had a wiener roast.

8 The fun seemed to last forever.

9 I'd like to return next year.

10 This could become our yearly outing!

Name: _____ **Date:** _____

Adjective or Adverb?

Directions: Decide if the word is an adjective or an adverb. Write it in the correct box.

Word Bank

already	awful	below	different	easily	exactly
fancy	gentle	greedy	greedily	outdoors	pleasant
quick	safely	sleepy	there	today	ugly

Adjectives (describe nouns)	Adverbs (often end in -ly and tell when, where, or how)

Name: _____ **Date:** _____

Making Words Plural

Directions: Most nouns become plurals by adding the letter *s* to the ends of the nouns. Write the plurals of the nouns below.

1 boy

_____

2 nickel

_____

3 treasure

_____

4 shirt

_____

5 giant

_____

6 spider

_____

Directions: Some words that end in *f* or *fe* form plurals by changing the *f* or *fe* to *-ves*. Write the plurals of the nouns below.

7 wife

_____

8 dwarf

_____

9 hoof

_____

10 leaf

_____

11 scarf

_____

12 elf

_____

Name: _____ **Date:** _____

Making More Words Plural

If the letter before the *y* is a consonant, the plural is formed by changing the *y* to *i* and adding *-es*.

Directions: Write the plurals of the nouns below.

1 baby		**2** fairy	
_____		_____	
3 study		**4** city	
_____		_____	
5 butterfly		**6** bunny	
_____		_____	
7 daddy		**8** company	
_____		_____	
9 candy		**10** patty	
_____		_____	
11 twenty		**12** strawberry	
_____		_____	

Name: _____ **Date:** _____

Making Words Plural with -*es*

Nouns ending in *s*, *sh*, *ch*, or *x* form plurals by adding -*es*.

Directions: Write the plurals of the nouns below.

1 kiss _____	**2** patch _____
3 church _____	**4** beach _____
5 coach _____	**6** six _____
7 wash _____	**8** crash _____
9 rich _____	**10** ax _____
11 pass _____	**12** scratch _____

Name: _____ **Date:** _____

Oh No! O-Word Plurals

Directions: If the letter before *o* is a consonant, often the plural is formed by adding *-es* to the word. Write the plurals of the nouns below.

1 hero

_____

2 volcano

_____

3 potato

_____

4 tomato

_____

5 echo

_____

6 zero

_____

Directions: Write the plurals of the nouns below.

7 cello

_____

8 tornado

_____

9 mango

_____

10 memo

_____

11 photo

_____

12 piano

_____

Name: _____ **Date:** _____

Sort the Nouns

> A **concrete noun** is something you can see or feel.
> *Bed* is a concrete noun.
>
> An **abstract noun** is an idea, event, or quality.
> *Sleep* is an abstract noun.

Directions: Look at the nouns below. Write each noun in the correct column.

Word Bank

ant	bowl	bravery	comfort	calendar
curiosity	difference	fear	flame	jar
knight	laughter	passenger	policeman	power
pride	rooster	shy	spoon	truth

Concrete Nouns	Abstract Nouns

Name: _____ **Date:** _____

More Noun Sorting

A **concrete noun** is something you can see or feel.
Friend is a concrete noun.

An **abstract noun** is an idea, event, or quality.
Friendship is an abstract noun.

Directions: Look at the nouns below. Write each noun in the correct column.

Word Bank

anger	apple	apron	barrel	bubble
cloth	dime	hive	honesty	hope
jewel	joy	knife	memory	pain
peace	sidewalk	thought	truth	worry

Concrete Nouns	Abstract Nouns

#50886—Bright & Brainy: 3rd Grade Practice

Name: _____ **Date:** _____

Verb Challenges!

Directions: Choose the correct form of past tense. Write it in the blank.

1 I _____ my sister to the fair.

   bringed   brought

2 I _____ her a bright red balloon.

   bought   buyed

3 She _____ red instead of blue.

   choosed   chose

4 We _____ caramel corn.

   ate   eated

5 She _____ my camera.

   borrowed   borrow

Name: _____ **Date:** _____

More Verb Challenges!

Directions: Choose the correct word to finish the story. *Hint*: All the words should be in past tense.

Word Bank

are	can't	couldn't	dreamed	go	got
had	has	is	said	says	talk
talked	take	took	was	went	were

Dream On!

Last night I _____ the most amazing

dream! I _____ that I _____

to the animal shelter to adopt a dog. When I got there,

all the cages _____ open. And the

animals all _____ like humans! One puppy

_____, "Take me home! I'm the perfect

pet!" Another puppy said, "No! Take me!" Each dog

_____ so cute. I

_____ make up my mind.

So I _____ five dogs

home! When I _____

home, what do you think my mom said?

Name: _____ **Date:** _____

Past, Present, or Future?

Verbs can tell when the action took place or will take place. Changing the ending on most verbs shows the tense.

Directions: Circle your answer and write the correct form of the verb on the line. Then, write if the action occurs in the past, present, or future.

---

1 Sharon (cooks, cooked, will cook) the soup this afternoon.

_____

2 Marty (chops, chopped, will chop) the vegetables this morning.

_____

3 Marie (shops, shopped, will shop) for fruit every day.

_____

4 We (need, needed, will need) to get the dessert made yesterday.

_____

5 I (bake, baked, will bake) the bread after the soup is ready.

_____

6 Can you (pick, picked, will pick) some flowers now?

_____

7 The soup (smells, smelled, will smell) perfect.

_____

8 I (add, added, will add) some salt to it a minute ago.

_____

9 Please (mix, mixed, will mix) the salad.

_____

10 I (clean, cleaned, will clean) up after dinner.

_____

Name: _____ **Date:** _____

More Past, Present, or Future?

Verbs can tell when the action took place or will take place. Changing the ending on most verbs shows the tense.

Directions: Circle your answer and write the correct form of the verb on the line. Then, write if the action occurs in the past, present, or future.

1 Joanne (opens, opened, will open) her gift yesterday.

_____

2 She (jumps, jumped, will jump) up and down. It was a new bike!

_____

3 Tomorrow Joanne (bikes, biked, will bike) to school.

_____

4 Irv (bikes, biked, will bike) with her tomorrow.

_____

5 Irv (fills, filled, will fill) his tires with air yesterday.

_____

6 Sometimes Irv (likes, liked, will like) to take the bus.

_____

7 Next week he (walks, walked, will walk) instead of riding.

_____

8 Joanne (walks, walked, will walk) with him later.

_____

9 I (wish, wished, will wish) I had a bike.

_____

10 For now, I (borrow, borrowed, will borrow) Joanne's bike.

_____

Name: _____ **Date:** _____

Be Agreeable!

Directions: Choose the correct verb.

1 Bees _____ very busy in the summer.

is   are

2 They _____ from flower to flower collecting pollen.

flies   fly

3 A bee _____ pollen on its legs.

collects   collect

4 Some bees _____ to just one kind of plant.

travels   travel

5 Sometimes crab spiders _____ in flowers.

hides   hide

6 They may _____ a bee.

captures   capture

7 The queen bee _____ very busy.

is   are

8 She may _____ 2,000 eggs in one day!

lays   lay

Name: _____ **Date:** _____

Be Agreeable Again!

. . . .

Directions: Choose the correct pronoun.

1 Parker should put away _____ papers.

his   their

2 All of the students should be in _____ seats by now.

his   their

3 I think that digging in the garden is hard on _____ knees.

my   our

4 Marcus chose football because he finds _____ fun.

it   them

5 Everybody needs to lower _____ voices.

her   their

6 Most dogs can find _____ bones.

his   their

7 Some of the players have on _____ helmets.

her   their

8 Most children do not like to get in _____ beds at night.

his   their

#50886—Bright & Brainy: 3rd Grade Practice   © Shell Education

Name: _____ **Date:** _____

Conjunction Junction!

A **conjunction** is a word that joins two or more words, phrases, or clauses.

Directions: Write a conjunction in each sentence. *Hint:* More than one choice may be correct.

Word Bank

and   but   nor   or   yet

1 Benjy _____ Carmel are our cousins.

2 My brother and I would like to see them a lot, _____ we live far apart.

3 It's always great when we go to their house _____ they come here.

4 Sometimes we call on the phone, _____ it's better to see each other.

5 When they come here, we ride bikes, swim, _____ take hikes.

6 When we go there, we jump on their trampoline, climb on the rocks nearby, _____ play hide _____ seek.

7 Neither Benjy _____ Carmel get to come here this summer.

8 We will miss them, _____ we get to see them during our winter break!

Name: _____ **Date:** _____

Subordinate Conjunctions!

Subordinate conjunctions join two parts of a sentence. They can show time, place, or cause and effect.

Directions: Write a subordinate conjunction in each sentence. *Hint*: More than one choice may be correct.

Word Bank

after	because	if	once	while
so that	whenever	where	whether	

❶ I will go to bed _____ I have my homework done.

❷ Mom will read me a story _____ I brush my teeth.

❸ I picked out a story _____ Jemmy got a drink of water.

❹ I like reading about kings and queens _____ they have castles.

❺ I'd like to be rich _____ I can have a castle.

❻ I choose books about castles _____ I go to the library.

❼ If I go to Europe I want to visit castles _____ I am there.

❽ Castles are fun to read about, _____ I get to visit one or not.

Name: _____ **Date:** _____

Keep It Simple!

> A **simple sentence** has a complete thought. It has a subject and a verb.

Directions: Write a *C* if the text is a complete sentence. Write an *I* if the text is a phrase.

_____ ❶ A baby has small bones.

_____ ❷ The strongest bone.

_____ ❸ By the time a body.

_____ ❹ Some bones grow together.

_____ ❺ With calcium bones and teeth.

_____ ❻ People can break their bones.

_____ ❼ Breaks and fractures of bones.

_____ ❽ It is important to drink milk.

_____ ❾ Helping bones with calcium.

_____ ❿ Bones never stop changing.

Directions: Finish the sentences below to make each a complete thought.

⓫ My bones _____

_____ .

⓬ My head _____

_____ .

Name: _____ **Date:** _____

Compound It!

. . . .

You can make a **compound sentence** by putting two complete thoughts together. The two complete thoughts are joined by a comma and the word *and* or *or*.

Directions: Join the sentences to make a compound sentence. Remember to add a comma before the *and* or *or*.

1 I want to take a walk. I want to see the sunset.

_____

_____

_____

2 I might watch a movie. I might play a video game.

_____

_____

_____

3 I walked into town. I stopped to see my friend.

_____

_____

_____

4 Mom said I could go to town. Mom said I could stay home.

_____

_____

_____

5 Do you like cats? Do you like dogs?

_____

_____

_____

Name: _____ **Date:** _____

Complex or Compound?

A **complex sentence** has an independent clause and a dependent clause. It is connected by words such as *although, after, as if, as soon as, before, because, if, since,* and *when*.

A **compound sentence** has two complete thoughts together. The two complete thoughts are joined by a comma and the word *and* or *or*.

Directions: Make a check by compound sentences. Make two checks by complex sentences.

_____ **1** As soon as I met him, I knew he would be my friend.

_____ **2** I liked his smile, and I liked his handshake.

_____ **3** When I went in the shop, she asked if I needed help.

_____ **4** Before we get started, let's see what we need to finish from yesterday.

_____ **5** I like to watch football, and I like to watch baseball.

_____ **6** Since I've been ten years old, I've enjoyed swimming.

_____ **7** Before I learned to swim, I was afraid of the water.

_____ **8** My gym teacher likes skiing, and my music teacher likes snowboarding.

_____ **9** Do you like downhill skiing, or do you like cross-country skiing?

_____ **10** When I got up this morning, I was really sleepy.

Name: _____ **Date:** _____

Simple, Compound, or Complex?

A **simple sentence** has one complete thought.

A **compound sentence** has two complete thoughts together. The two complete thoughts are joined by a comma and the word *and* or *or*.

A **complex sentence** has an independent clause and a dependent clause. It is connected by words such as *although, after, as if, as soon as, before, because, if, since,* and *when*.

Directions: Write an *S* if it is a simple sentence. Write a *C* if it is a compound sentence. Write two Cs by the complex sentences.

_____ **1** The sun shines down on the city.

_____ **2** Yesterday there was thunder and lightning.

_____ **3** After seeing the sun come out, we thought we'd have a picnic.

_____ **4** Although there is a chance of rain, it seems we'll have good weather.

_____ **5** Do you like rain, or do you like sun?

_____ **6** Since I've moved to the mountains, I don't mind the rain.

_____ **7** When I lived by the ocean, I liked the sunshine best.

_____ **8** I would swim every day.

_____ **9** As soon as the sun rose, I'd be at the beach.

_____ **10** Although I miss the ocean, I love the mountains.

Name: _____ **Date:** _____

Movies, Songs, and Plays

Directions: Rewrite each sentence to capitalize the proper nouns that name movies, songs, television shows, and plays.

1 My favorite movie is free willy.

_____

_____

_____

2 Would you like to sing the itsy bitsy spider with me?

_____

_____

_____

3 We learned to sing down by the station in kindergarten.

_____

_____

_____

4 My sister loves to watch barney and friends.

_____

_____

_____

5 We have all the home alone movies.

_____

_____

_____

Name: _____ **Date:** _____

Books and Capitals!

Directions: Rewrite each sentence to capitalize the proper nouns that name books. Be sure to underline the titles, too.

1 My favorite book is the wonderful wizard of oz.

_____

_____

_____

2 Dad has been reading twenty thousand leagues under the sea.

_____

_____

_____

3 Mom said her favorite book is the secret garden.

_____

_____

_____

4 When I was little, she read goodnight moon to me every night.

_____

_____

_____

5 Books like pippi longstocking have been made into movies.

_____

_____

_____

Name: _____ **Date:** _____

Addressing an Envelope

You may need to write an address in several places: the heading of a letter, on an envelope, or when filling out a form. Use a comma to separate the city and state.

Darren Westfield
123 East Willow Avenue
Pike, CO 82220

Return address
(name and address of
sender)

stamp

Mark Matthews
992 Feather Lane, Apt. 3B
Winslow, IL 60001

Address of recipient

Directions: Use your name and address as the return address. Make up the name and address of a recipient. Then, design a stamp.

Name: _____ Date: _____

It's Quotable!

Use **quotation marks** around a **direct quote**. Use a **comma** to set off a quotation.

Example: Dad said, "Take out the trash."

Directions: Put a comma and quotation marks in each sentence.

1 The man said You can line up now.

2 Nathan said I can't believe we are going on the roller coaster.

3 The woman said Fasten your seat belts.

4 Jefferson said This is the first time I've ridden a roller coaster.

5 Nathan said Wow! This is really fast!

6 Jefferson screamed I think I want off this roller coaster!

7 Nathan shouted Hang on! It's fun!

8 Jefferson answered Whee! I hope this is the last time around!

9 The woman announced Stay seated until the ride stops.

10 Jefferson asked Can we do it again?

Name: _____ **Date:** _____

In Need of Quotes!

Use **quotation marks** around a **direct quote**. Use a **comma** to set off a quotation.

Example: Terry said, "May I go with you?"

Directions: Practice using quotation marks and commas by choosing a sentence to complete each blank.

Sentence Bank	
Watch out!	Is that a ghost?
It's a cat.	Don't be a baby.
What's behind the door?	Everywhere we go, we see them.
I really like snakes.	I don't ever want to see that again.
Let's go!	Take me along.

1 Robin called, _____

2 Patsy replied, _____

3 _____ asked Trent.

4 _____ Patsy screamed.

Name: _____ **Date:** _____

Who Owns That?

An **apostrophe** is used to show possession. That means something is owned.

Example: John's hat means the hat belongs to John.

Directions: Add an apostrophe to show ownership.

1 the farmer's plow

2 the cows stall

3 the horses saddle

4 the chickens roost

5 the calfs tail

Directions: Show possession in the following phrases. Use an apostrophe.

6 the stable belonging to a horse

_____

_____

7 the wheel belonging to a wagon_____

_____

_____

8 the plants belonging in a garden_____

_____

_____

Name: _____ **Date:** _____

Plural or Possession?

Directions: If the underlined word shows ownership, add an apostrophe. If it is a plural word, do not add an apostrophe.

1 The <u>dinosaurs</u> skull is huge.

2 <u>Dinosaurs</u> lived millions of years ago.

3 One <u>museums</u> display has four dinosaur skeletons.

4 Most <u>scientists</u> think the *Troodon* was the smartest dinosaur.

5 A dinosaur <u>adults</u> lifespan could have been more than 100 years.

6 A dinosaur may be named after its <u>bodys</u> feature.

7 A dinosaur may be named after a <u>scientists</u> name.

8 Dinosaurs became extinct about 65 million <u>years</u> ago.

9 Some dinosaurs ate <u>plants</u>, <u>leaves</u>, <u>ferns</u> or <u>mosses</u>.

10 Other dinosaurs ate <u>animals</u> eggs.

Name: _____ **Date:** _____

Meet the OO Families

Directions: Some groups of words have the same spelling pattern. They belong to a word "family." Read the words. Write them in the column.

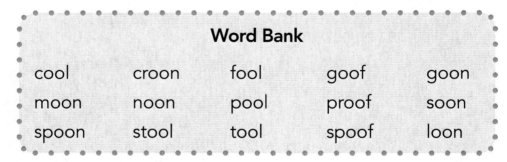

Word Bank

cool	croon	fool	goof	goon
moon	noon	pool	proof	soon
spoon	stool	tool	spoof	loon

-ool family	*-oon* family	*-oof* family

Name: _____ **Date:** _____

Meet Some Letter Patterns

Directions: Look at the words. They will help you spell the word for the picture. Write the word under each picture.

1 fowl

howl

_____

2 blouse

mouse

_____

3 blush

crush

_____

4 seas

fleas

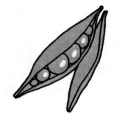

_____

5 blue

clue

_____

6 brain

drain

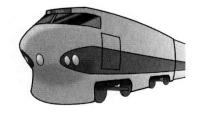

_____

Name: _____ **Date:** _____

Take Position!

Directions: Look at the words. They will help you spell the word for the picture. Write the word under each picture.

❶ hall

mall

_____

❷ sell

tell

_____

❸ stand

land

_____

❹ hair

fair

_____

❺ munch

crunch

_____

❻ steal

deal

_____

Name: _____ **Date:** _____

Take Note of K!

Directions: Look at the pictures. Say the word. Then, spell the word.

1

_____

2

_____

3

_____

4

_____

5

_____

6
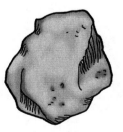

_____

   57

Name: _____ **Date:** _____

Syllable Ending Rules

Directions: Look at the pictures. Say the word. Then, spell the word.

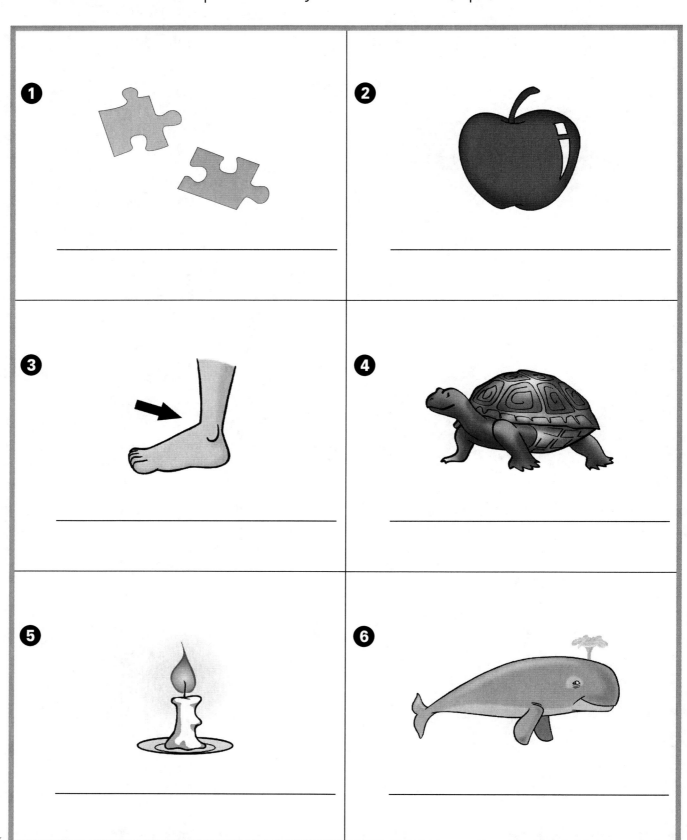

① _____

② _____

③ _____

④ _____

⑤ _____

⑥ _____

Name: _____ **Date:** _____

More Syllable Ending Rules

When adding *-tion* to a word that ends in *-e*, drop the *e*.
Example: collaborate, collaboration

When adding *-tion* to a word that ends in *t*, do not double the *t*.
Example: act, action

Directions: Look at the words below. Add *-tion* to each word.

1 coordinate _____

2 collect _____

3 communicate _____

4 construct _____

5 correct _____

6 create _____

7 decorate _____

8 direct _____

9 educate _____

10 elect _____

11 inspect _____

12 instruct _____

Name: _____ Date: _____

Hinky Pinky Fun!

Hinky pinkies are words that rhyme and have the same number of syllables in each word. They are fun to do with riddles.

Example: What would you call a tardier crocodile-like animal?

Later gator

Directions: Figure out the hinky pinkies. Remember, the answers must rhyme.

1 What would you call someone who brags about a kitchen appliance?

_____

2 What would you call someone who lives in a basement?

_____

3 What would you call a chillier paper holder?

_____

4 What would you call someone who blocks a kangaroo?

_____

5 What would you call a bloody tale?

_____

6 What would you call a clever detective?

_____

7 What would you call an unpredictable gherkin?

_____

8 What would you call a clever large community?

_____

Name: _____ Date: _____

Parts Count!

Directions: Read the information about the word parts in the first box. Then, choose the best word to finish each sentence from the Word Bank.

Word Parts	Word Bank
aqua means *water*	aquatics
duct means *lead*	conducts
loc means *place*	location
multi means *many*	multiple
opt means *best*	optimal
port means *carry*	transportation
rupt means *break*	interruption
struct means *build*	structure

1 We went swimming at the _____ center.

2 They have a new _____ downtown.

3 It is the _____ place for swimming lessons.

4 The _____ is huge.

5 There are _____ lesson times.

6 We can get there using public _____ .

7 Miss Gonzalez _____ the class.

8 Our lesson lasts one hour with one short _____ .

Name: _____ **Date:** _____

Find and Spell

> **tongs**—tool for picking up something
>
> **tongue**—the movable part of the mouth used to taste
>
> **tonnage**—total weight in tons shipped
>
> **tonsils**—a pair of masses of tissue at the back of the mouth
>
> **toolshed**—a small building for storing tools
>
> **toothpick**—a pointed tool for removing food from between the teeth
>
> **topknot**—a tuft of feathers on top of the head
>
> **topsy-turvy**—upside down

Directions: Choose the correct word from the partial dictionary entries.

1 He lifted the corn out with _____.

2 After eating corn on the cob I need a _____ for my teeth.

3 The cat lapped up the water with its _____.

4 The ship can carry more _____ than the barge.

5 I had a sore throat and had to have my _____ removed.

6 The funny bird had a _____ on its head.

7 That was a _____ roller coaster ride!

8 Please put the rake and the shovel in the _____.

#50886—Bright & Brainy: 3rd Grade Practice   © Shell Education

Name: _____ **Date:** _____

What Word?

Directions: Choose a word for *wet* and a word for *precipitation* for each sentence. *Hint:* There is more than one answer for some sentences.

Wet		Precipitation	
clammy	misty	cloudburst	fog
damp	soaked	deluge	rain
humid	sodden	downpour	rainstorm
moist	steamy	drizzle	shower

1 My raincoat felt _____ in the _____.

2 The grey _____ made everything _____.

3 The jungle was _____ because of the long _____.

4 I got absolutely _____ in the _____.

5 The weather can be _____ even if there isn't a _____.

6 The sudden _____ left everything _____.

Name: _____ **Date:** _____

Choosing Words

Directions: Match the words to the nouns below to create an interesting image.
Hint: There can be more than one good choice.

Word Bank

billowy	bitter	brilliant	cuddly	crackling	craggy
dusky	elegant	filthy	gigantic	graceful	greasy
hazy	hushed	motionless	musty	revolting	rippling
sour	stale	sticky	tart		

1 _____ dancer

2 _____ fried chicken

3 _____ toddlers

4 _____ beggars

5 _____ singer

6 _____ waterfall

7 _____ taffy

8 _____ friend

9 _____ aunt

10 _____ flowers

11 _____ peaches

12 _____ attic

Name: _____ **Date:** _____

Get a Clue!

Have you ever been told to "Get a clue?" That is an informal way of saying to act or speak more thoughtfully.

Directions: Rewrite these sentences using formal English. The informal English words or phrases are in bold.

1 I've been feeling **blue** today.

_____

_____

2 That costs 100 **bucks.**

_____

_____

3 **Buzz off!**

_____

_____

4 I'll **keep my fingers crossed** for you.

_____

_____

5 I need to **learn it by heart**.

_____

_____

6 **Hold your horses!**

_____

_____

Name: _____ **Date:** _____

Informal and Formal English

Directions: Draw a line to connect the word with the correct meaning.

1 nope		when everything goes wrong
2 lovey-dovey		yes
3 bad hair day		lose your temper
4 cakewalk		between gigantic and enormous
5 buzz off		anything you can't recall the name of
6 uh-huh		no
7 ginormous		tease
8 jerk your chain		go away
9 blow a fuse		romantic
10 thingamajigger		easily done

Name: _____ **Date:** _____

The White Mouse

Directions: Read the article. Then, answer the questions on the next page.

To Spy or Not to Spy?

Have you ever thought about being a spy? Nancy Wake had not planned to be a spy. She lived in France during World War II. France was under the control of Germany. Nancy and her husband were very rich. They used their money to help airmen escape. Nancy wanted to help more. She was very good at disguises. And she was very hard to catch. Her name became the White Mouse.

Things got worse in France. Nancy had to escape to Spain. She was caught during one try. But she was let go. She tried again and got to Great Britain. She worked as a nurse. She was really getting ready to parachute back into France. She wanted to help organize people and fight against the Germans. She even led raids against the Germans.

Nancy was thrilled when the war ended. Then, she learned about her husband. He had stayed in France. He was captured and killed. He paid the ultimate price for helping the French people.

The White Mouse *(cont.)*

1 How does Nancy Wake and her husband help during World War II?

   a. They give their money to the French soldiers.

   b. They help people escape.

   c. They make weapons for the French.

2 Why does Nancy Wake become a spy?

   a. She wants to fight the Germans.

   b. She likes wearing disguises.

   c. She lives in France.

3 Why do you think she has to escape to Spain?

   a. They are running out of money.

   b. It is getting dangerous in France.

   c. She wants to travel.

4 Why do you think she works as a nurse?

   a. She needs a job to raise more money.

   b. She likes helping people.

   c. The job kept people from knowing she is a spy.

5 Why do you think the title is "The White Mouse"?

   a. Because Nancy is hard to catch.

   b. Because Nancy likes mice.

   c. Because spies are called by animal names.

Name: _____ **Date:** _____

Achoooo!

Directions: Read the article. Then, answer the questions on the next page.

Stay Healthy!

Catching a chill does not mean you will catch a cold. Having wet hair does not give you a cold. Something you can't even see gives you that dreaded cold. It's called a virus. A virus is a kind of germ. The one that gives us colds is called the rhinovirus.

There are several ways to get that virus. You might touch something that has the virus on it. You might be near someone with a cold who sneezes. It doesn't take long for the virus to affect you. That virus might get started within 15 minutes! Soon you might have a sore throat or a drippy nose.

Once you get a cold, drink lots of water and fruit juices. Rest a lot. Cover your nose and mouth when you sneeze. Wash your hands a lot. That helps keep you from passing it along to someone else. Finally, remind yourself that a cold lasts about a week. You'll soon feel better.

Achoooo! *(cont.)*

1 What is a virus?

    a. It's a cold.

    b. It's a germ.

    c. It's a flu bug.

2 How might you get a cold?

    a. from having wet hair

    b. from being outside too much

    c. from touching something with the virus

3 How do you know you probably have a cold?

    a. You want to drink lots of fruit juices.

    b. You touched something with the rhinovirus.

    c. You have a sore throat.

4 What are two important things to do when you get a cold?

    a. Eat toast with honey and drink milk.

    b. Get plenty of exercise and limit sweets.

    c. Get plenty of rest and drink liquids.

5 According to the article, which sentence is true?

    a. You shouldn't go outside during cold season.

    b. You shouldn't eat and drink too much.

    c. You should try to not pass along the virus.

Name: _____ **Date:** _____

Get to High Ground!

Directions: Read the article. Then, answer the questions on the next page.

River Danger

Taking a vacation by a river can be a great time. That's what more than 3,000 tourists thought on July 31, 1976. They were by the Big Thompson River in Colorado. It is in the foothills of the Rocky Mountains. The river flows down a beautiful canyon. And the summer weather is usually warm and sunny. It is a great place for river sports and enjoying the mountains.

But that all changed on July 31 in 1976. Strong thunderstorms moved in. Heavy rain fell for four-and-a-half hours that evening. The river is usually one or two feet deep. The canyon is 25 miles long. But it is narrow. There wasn't anywhere for the water to go—except up the walls of the canyon.

Flash floods began. Some people said they saw a wall of water eight feet high. It was hard to warn people. Some didn't believe that there could be a bad flood there. But the flooding was devastating. 139 people died. More than 300 homes were destroyed. Only getting to high ground saved many people from drowning.

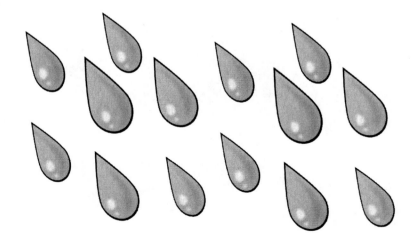

Get to High Ground! *(cont.)*

1 Why do so many tourists go to the Big Thompson River?

    a. They want to enjoy the river.

    b. They want to see flash floods.

    c. They want to help save people.

2 What plays a part in the flooding?

    a. hail and lightning, combined with poor communication

    b. warm weather and rain, combined with too many people

    c intense thunderstorms, combined with a narrow canyon

3 What does "wall of water" mean?

    a. a wall from a building being pushed down the river

    b. water that comes in a series of waves

    c. water that has built up very high as it moves

4 Why do some people die?

    a. They do not believe the warnings that a flood was coming.

    b. They like swimming in the river.

    c. They make it to high ground.

5 What should you do when near a river?

    a. have fun and not worry unless you get a warning of a flood

    b. pay attention to the weather and be prepared for danger

    c. camp where you can see if a flood is coming

Name: _____ **Date:** _____

Up You Go!

Directions: Read the article. Then, answer the questions on the next page.

Climbing to the Top

Do you want to climb up a wall like Spiderman? There is a way. This sport is called indoor rock climbing. Climbing walls can be found in gyms in many towns and cities. The climbing wall has handholds built into the walls. Routes—different ways up the walls—can be easy or difficult.

But before you start climbing that wall, you'll need training. You'll learn about all the gear you'll use, such as climbing shoes and helmets. You'll learn how to put on the safety harness. You'll also learn how to use the ropes. Once you are ready, you'll need someone to hold the ropes or belay. This person holds the ropes and makes sure you don't fall far if you slip.

Indoor climbing helps build strong muscles. Many people enjoy it. Even preschoolers climb rock walls! It's a great way to have fun and get exercise at the same time!

Up You Go! *(cont.)*

1 Why do people climb walls at gyms?

   a. for fun and exercise

   b. to be a super hero

   c. to hold ropes

2 Why do you need training?

   a. so you can teach climbing

   b. so you can climb alone

   c. so you can climb safely

3 What do you need to climb at a climbing gym?

   a. loose clothing and tennis shoes

   b. shoes, helmet, and a safety harness

   c. ropes and climbing boots

4 Which sentence is true?

   a. The belayer holds the ropes while you climb.

   b. Only small children can climb.

   c. You need to be strong before you start climbing.

5 Where would a good place be to find a climbing wall?

   a. in the mountains

   b. at a recreation center or gym

   c. at an amusement park

Name: _____ **Date:** _____

Dusty Storms

Directions: Read the article. Then, answer the questions on the next page.

Storm Alert!

Dust storms don't just happen in a desert. They can happen in any dry area. They just need two things: lots of sand or dust and a strong wind. You might think that if there's no sand or dust near you that you're safe from a dust storm. However, strong winds can blow a dust storm thousands of miles.

Dust storms can be very dangerous. They make it hard to see. They can damage cars. They can cause erosion. That means that the top soil blows away. The wind can spin and make funnels something like tornados. They are called dust devils. They can be seen on Mars!

Some of the ways to stay safe are the same as during a blizzard. Stay inside and keep your doors and windows closed. If you are outside, cover your mouth and eyes. Get to a safe place as soon as possible.

Dusty Storms *(cont.)*

1 What is needed for a dust storm?

   a. a desert, river, and strong winds

   b. a dry area with sand or dust and wind

   c. erosion, dirt, and a strong wind

2 You might experience a dust storm anywhere. Why?

   a. Dust storms can turn into blizzards.

   b. Winds can spin dust storms like tornados.

   c. Winds can blow dust storms thousands of miles.

3 What is erosion?

   a. the process of top soil getting worn down

   b. the process of dust blowing away

   c. the process of top soil getting dust added

4 How is a dust devil formed?

   a. The winds from Mars blow in Earth's deserts.

   b. The winds blow across deserts.

   c. The winds spin the dirt in a circular fashion.

5 What is the main idea of this story?

   a. Dust storms can affect anyone, anywhere.

   b. Dust storms are a lot like blizzards.

   c. Dust storms can be seen on Mars.

Name: _____ **Date:** _____

NASA at Work

Directions: Read the article. Then, answer the questions on the next page.

Amazing NASA

You may not think that what happens in outer space affects you.
But it does! NASA stands for the National Aeronautics and Space
Administration. They run the space program. They make a lot of new
things to help with space travel. You may want to use some of them.

NASA has to polish the mirrors used in their telescopes. This tool is
perfect for polishing ice skate blades. It makes them go really fast!
Did you ever get tired of taking pills when you were sick? NASA made
a small gadget that can be put right inside your body. It gives you the
right amount of medicine when you need it. Another kind of pill lets
the doctor check your temperature from inside your body!

NASA has made amazing robots, too. Soon they might help with your
chores. Someday you'll be able to move your hand to control a game
on your computer screen. When that day comes, you can thank NASA!

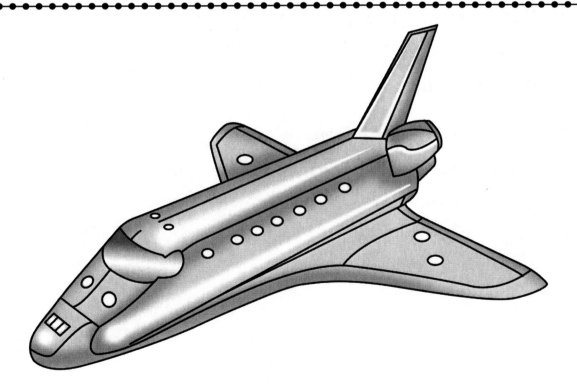

NASA at Work (cont.)

1 Why does NASA create new things?

   a. They have inventors creating things.

   b. They create products to sell.

   c. They create products for the space program.

2 How does NASA help ice skaters?

   a. They developed a polishing tool.

   b. They developed amazing mirrors.

   c. They developed ice skate blades.

3 How does NASA help doctors?

   a. Their tools help doctors do operations.

   b. Their tools help doctors treat patients.

   c. Their tools help doctors do experiments.

4 Why is NASA important to you?

   a. They create useful tools.

   b. They help you play games.

   c. They train astronauts.

5 What is the main idea of this article?

   a. NASA stands for the National Aeronautics and Space Administration.

   b. Tools developed for the space program are useful on Earth, too.

   c. NASA invents tools for the space program.

Name: _____ **Date:** _____

Power Up with a Nap!

Directions: Read the article. Then, answer the questions on the next page.

Take a Break!

Have you ever wondered why you get sleepy? Your body is an amazing machine. But it needs sleep—and food—to keep going. Newborn babies usually sleep 15 or 16 hours a day. The rest of the time they are probably eating—or crying! All that sleeping and eating gives the body the fuel it needs to grow.

How do you know it's time to get some sleep? Your eyes might feel heavy. It gets harder to think clearly. You might really want to finish the book or game. But your mind isn't letting you. It just wants a break from running your body. Then it can dream or think about the day while you sleep.

By the time you are an adult, eight hours of sleep is about right. But people have learned that a short nap during the day really helps. It just takes about 20 minutes to feel powered up and ready to work again. Some companies have created "quiet rooms" that are perfect for a "power" nap. So the next time you feel drowsy, give yourself the break you need!

Power Up with a Nap! *(cont.)*

1 Why do newborn babies sleep so much?

  a. They get tired from eating and crying.

  b. They are too little to do anything else.

  c. They are growing a lot.

2 Why do you get sleepy?

  a. Your body needs a rest.

  b. Your brain needs to run your body.

  c. Your brain wants to work.

3 How long of a nap do you need each day?

  a. about 15 hours

  b. about 20 minutes

  c. about 12 hours

4 Why do some companies have quiet rooms?

  a. Naps help people work better.

  b. Naps waste time.

  c. Naps need to last at least an hour.

5 What is the main idea of this article?

  a. Your brain works and dreams while you sleep.

  b. You are going to get sleepy each day.

  c. Sleep gives your body the break it needs.

Name: _____ **Date:** _____

Sleep Tight!

Directions: Read the article. Then, answer the questions on the next page.

Cozy Sleep

Has anyone ever said, "Good night! Sleep tight! Don't let the bedbugs bite!?" It is easy to understand that last part about the bedbugs. No one wants to get bitten by anything during the night! But what does *sleep tight* mean?

There are two possible meanings for *sleep tight.* One meaning is that *sleep tight* simply means to sleep well. The other meaning comes from the structure of beds. In the 1600s, beds were made with wood and ropes. The frame was built of wood. The side rails of the bed had holes in them. Ropes were stretched across from side to side and pulled through the holes. The mattress, which might be filled with straw or wool, was placed on the ropes.

Beds weren't as big as they are today. In many homes, several children would share a bed. After a while, the ropes would stretch and the mattress would sag. So the ropes would need to be tightened. In wealthy homes, that job fell to the servants.

Now when you go to sleep on a comfy bed, be glad that you can *sleep tight*!

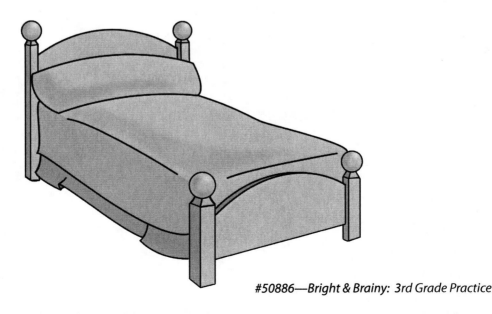

Sleep Tight! *(cont.)*

1 Why would someone say, "Don't let the bedbugs bite?"

   a. Bedbugs live in straw mattresses.

   b. Bedbugs can bite sleepers.

   c. Bedbugs are like spiders.

2 What does "the structure of beds" mean?

   a. how beds were made

   b. how mattresses were made

   c. how people slept in beds

3 How do the ropes work?

   a. They hold the frame together.

   b. They hold the rails together.

   c. They hold the mattress.

4 Why do the ropes sag?

   a. The weight of the sleepers stretch them.

   b. Servants tighten them in wealthy homes.

   c. The mattress are made of straw.

5 What is the main idea of the article?

   a. the meaning of *don't let the bedbugs bite*

   b. the possible meanings of *sleep tight*

   c. how to have a good night's sleep

Name: _____ **Date:** _____

The Great American Desert

Directions: Read the article. Then, match each word to its definition.

Desert Exploration

If you lived in the United States in the 1800s, you didn't know much about the West. That changed after President Thomas Jefferson sent Zebulon M. Pike to explore the area. Pike wrote a book about what he saw. He wrote about the mountains. He wrote about the Indian tribes he'd met. He even told about hunting for buffalo!

People wondered if this would be a good place to live. Stephen H. Long came with some men to explore. It was a hot summer. The plains were barren, with sand blowing. He said that no one would want to reside in the "Great American Desert!" Of course they did move there. These people live in Colorado!

---

1 explore   groups of people

2 tribes   empty

3 buffalo   investigate

4 barren   live

5 reside   dry region

6 desert   bison

Name: _____ **Date:** _____

Gold Fever

Directions: Read the article. Then, match each word to its definition.

Gold Rush

During the mid-1800s, many people caught gold fever. They rushed west to search for gold. Life was rugged. Miners carried a lot of equipment with them to get started. They also brought some food. Once at a mining site, a miner might sleep in a tent or just in a bedroll. When they ran out of food, they needed to buy more provisions.

Getting supplies to the miners was a big job. Horses, mules, or oxen pulled wagons. When the wagons got to the steep mountains, they'd stop. The supplies were loaded onto pack horses or burros. Once those got over the mountains, the supplies would be taken to storekeepers in mining towns. The lucky miners would have enough gold dust or nuggets to buy what they needed.

❶ equipment		supplies
❷ rugged		gear, tools
❸ site		high, vertical
❹ bedroll		rough
❺ provisions		blanket
❻ steep		place

Name: _____ **Date:** _____

The American Eagle

Directions: Read the article. Then, match each word to its definition.

Bald Eagle

One of the most famous symbols in America is the bald eagle. The eagle is a good choice. It's a powerful bird. The female eagle may weigh 14 pounds. Her wingspan may be eight feet! Eagles mate for life. They build huge nests for their eaglets. The nest may weigh one ton!

Bald eagles can fly 30 miles per hour. They can dive faster, especially if they are grabbing a fish out of the water. The eagle isn't really bald. Its name comes from piebald, which means two colors. When the eagle became our national symbol, they were easy to see in the sky. Then they began to die off. Now laws protect them.

---

1 symbol   baby eagles

2 wingspan   partner

3 mate   representation

4 eaglets   guard

5 national   length from tip to tip

6 protect   countrywide

Name: _____ **Date:** _____

A Great Lady

Directions: Read the article. Then, match each word to its definition.

The Statue of Liberty

Thousands of immigrants came to the United States by ship. They would wait impatiently for their first sight of a great lady. That lady is the Statue of Liberty. Seeing the statue meant their journey was nearly done. They would soon start their new lives.

The Statue of Liberty was a gift. It was made in France. Then, it was packed into more than 200 crates. It took four months to reassemble it. The crown on her head has seven rays. They represent the seven continents and the seven seas. The torch stands for freedom. The statue is more than 300 feet high from the ground to the torch. The statue was dedicated in 1886. It still stands for freedom and our friendship with France.

---

1 immigrants

2 impatiently

3 journey

4 crates

5 reassemble

6 represent

trip

stand for

settlers, newcomers

put together

wooden boxes

eagerly

Name: _____ **Date:** _____

Sidebar Skills

A **sidebar** is a box with some useful information. It usually goes with a longer article.

Directions: Read each sidebar. Then, answer the questions.

Fast Facts	
Tyrannosaurus Rex	
Height	15–20 feet
Length	40 feet
Length of jaw	4 feet
Length of arms	3 feet

1 What can you learn about the Tyrannosaurus Rex by reading this sidebar?

_____

_____

Fast Facts

***Triceratops Horridus'* Diet**

- ferns
- cycads
- palms

2 What can you learn about the Triceratops Horridus by reading this sidebar?

_____

_____

Name: _____ **Date:** _____

More Sidebar Skills

A **sidebar** is a box with some useful information. It usually goes with a longer article.

Directions: Read each sidebar. Then, answer the questions.

Are Constellations Real?

Constellations are not real. They are made up to help us find our way around the sky. It's easy to find the Big Dipper or the Great Bear. Its formal name is Ursa Major. Once you find the Big Dipper, you can find the North Star. Each map or image, such as Orion, serves as a guide.

❶ What can you learn by reading this sidebar?

_____

_____

_____

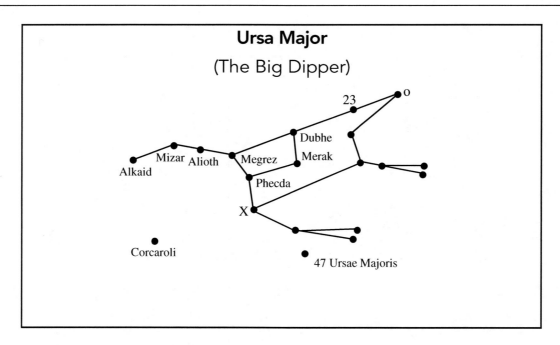

Ursa Major

(The Big Dipper)

❷ What can you tell by looking at this sidebar?

_____

_____

_____

Name: _____ **Date:** _____

Diagram Smarts

A **diagram** is an illustration with information. It usually goes with a longer article.

Directions: Read each diagram. Then, answer the questions.

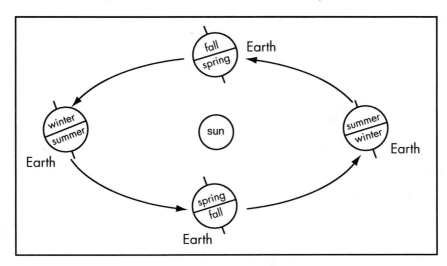

1 What can you learn from this diagram?

_____

_____

_____

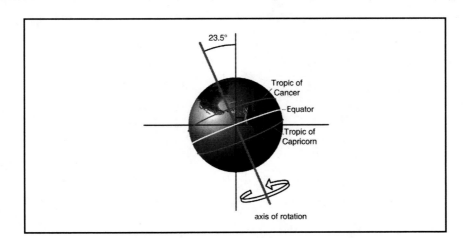

2 What can you learn from this diagram?

_____

_____

_____

Name: _____ **Date:** _____

More Diagrams

> A **sidebar** is a box with some useful information. It usually goes with a longer article.

Directions: Read each sidebar. Then, answer the questions.

Water Usage	
Taking a shower	7 gallons per minute
Bath	28–36 gallons to fill
Running faucet	3 gallons per minute
Washing machine	30–40 gallons per load
Dishwasher	15–20 gallons per load
Watering lawn	3–5 gallons per minute
Flushing toilet	6 gallons per flush

❶ What can you learn from this sidebar?

_____

_____

_____

Saving Water	
• Take shorter showers.	• Wash full loads of laundry.
• Don't fill the bathtub.	• Change to drip systems. Have less grass.
• Turn off the faucet quickly.	• Change to low-flush toilets.
• Wash full loads of dishes.	

❷ What can you learn from this sidebar?

_____

_____

_____

Name: _____ **Date:** _____

The Only Place to Live

Directions: Each of these two writers has a different point of view. Read what they have written. Then, answer the questions.

Passage 1

There is nothing better than waking up to the sound of the waves. That's why I'll always choose the beach as my favorite place to live. If I want to swim, surf, or fish, all I have to do is pull on my swimsuit, put on sunscreen, grab my gear, and head out the door. I know the ocean isn't for everyone. I'm glad! That means that there are fewer people getting in my way on a sunny, hot day.

1 What does this person think about living by the ocean?

_____

_____

_____

_____

Passage 2

I would never want to live by the ocean. Every time there is a bad storm, people have to board up their homes. They have to leave everything behind sometimes. Shark attacks may be rare. But I still worry about them. It can cost a lot to live by the ocean. I would rather save that money and just have my vacations there.

2 What does this person think about living by the ocean?

_____

_____

_____

_____

Name: _____ **Date:** _____

The Best Pet

Directions: Each of these two writers has a different point of view. Read what they have written. Then, answer the questions.

Passage 1

You might think I'm going to say that a dog or a cat makes the best pet. You'd be wrong. The best pet in the world is a bull snake. They aren't poisonous. They easily get used to being handled. It's interesting to feel their muscles as they move when you hold them. They don't take up much space. You just need a 20 gallon tank, a rock for them to lie on, some water, and food. When you're ready for a pet, choose a bull snake!

---

❶ What does this person think about having a bull snake as a pet?

_____

_____

_____

_____

Passage 2

A bull snake is not a good choice for a pet. They can get used to being handled. That's true. However, they can be aggressive and act just like a rattlesnake. They can grow to be six feet long. That is a lot of snake to handle. And don't forget that you have to feed them live mice. That's not comfortable for a lot of people to do. I'd rather have that mouse for a pet than let it become snake food!

---

❷ What does this person think about having a bull snake as a pet?

_____

_____

_____

_____

Name: _____ **Date:** _____

Junk Food in Schools

Directions: Each of these two writers has a different point of view. Read what they have written. Then, answer the questions.

Passage 1

Junk food has no place in schools. Too many people are overweight. School is the best place to learn about eating the right foods. Many school lunch programs are changing. Instead of fried chicken, they serve grilled chicken. Why would they also have junk food around? It is time to get junk food out of schools!

---

1 What does this person think about having junk food in schools?

_____

_____

_____

_____

Passage 2

Having poor eating habits is a problem. But banning junk food from schools is not going to fix it. If kids can't get a treat in school, they will just get it after school. Eating the right food at lunch is a start. But the real answer is education. Kids have to learn the importance of eating the right foods. Having a chocolate bar is fine if it's just once in a while.

---

2 What does this person think about having junk food in schools?

_____

_____

_____

Name: _____ **Date:** _____

Chores

Directions: Each of these two writers has a different point of view. Read what they have written. Then, answer the questions.

Passage 1

Kids shouldn't get paid for doing chores around the house. It's part of being in a family. No one is paying parents for doing dishes or laundry. Things need to be cleaned. Meals need to be prepared. Everything runs more smoothly if everyone pitches in and helps.

---

❶ What does this person think about getting paid for doing chores?

_____

_____

_____

_____

Passage 2

Kids are very busy before and after school. They have more homework than ever. When kids have chores too, they tend to put them off. Parents have to nag them. That's not good for anyone. Adults get paid for their jobs. Kids should get paid for chores, too.

---

❷ What does this person think about getting paid for doing chores?

_____

_____

_____

_____

Name: _____ **Date:** _____

Can You Hear It?

Directions: Study the illustration. Then, answer the questions.

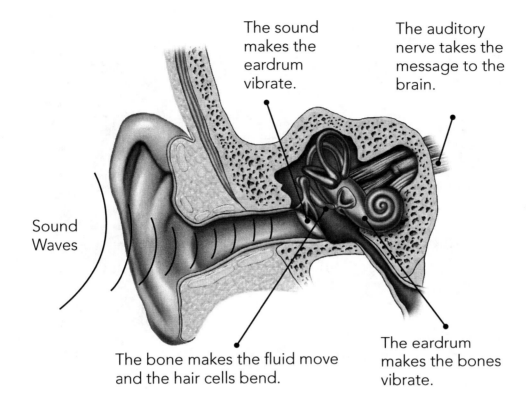

The sound makes the eardrum vibrate.

The auditory nerve takes the message to the brain.

Sound Waves

The bone makes the fluid move and the hair cells bend.

The eardrum makes the bones vibrate.

1 What moves into the outer ear?

_____

2 What happens to the eardrum when the sound reaches it?

_____

3 What makes the bones vibrate?

_____

4 What do the bones do?

_____

5 What does the auditory nerve do?

_____

Name: _____ **Date:** _____

Can You Smell It?

· ·

Directions: Study the illustration. Then, answer the questions below.

The **olfactory bulb** is responsible for identifying different scents.

Mucus membranes line and protect the inside of your nose.

Nose hairs help protect the body from germs, fungus, and spores.

Cilia are tiny hairs that help move mucus out of the lungs.

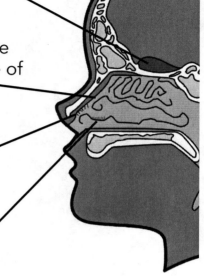

❶ What does the cilia do?

_____

_____

❷ What is the difference between nose hairs and cilia?

_____

_____

❸ What does the olfactory bulb do?

_____

_____

Name: _____ **Date:** _____

Clean Streets!

Directions: Read the article. Then, answer the questions.

Street Cleaning

Ben Franklin lived in Philadelphia for years. The streets were mostly packed dirt. There were bricks in the middle of the streets. But there weren't enough of them. Dust would pile up. It blew into homes and shops. When it rained, the mud was terrible.

Ben had a good idea. First, he got some people to pay a small amount each month to get the streets swept. Second, he wrote an article about the benefits of regular morning sweeping. The shops and houses were cleaner. Soon everyone wanted clean streets. It was easy to get a tax passed for street cleaning.

❶ Ben Franklin recognized a problem. What is it?

_____

_____

_____

❷ Ben Franklin took two important steps. What are they?

_____

_____

_____

❸ What is the result of his steps?

_____

_____

Name: _____ **Date:** _____

Ping...Ping...Ping...

Directions: Read the article. Then, answer the questions.

SONAR

Have you ever seen the ocean? It can be very deep. Whole mountains are under the waves in some places. People needed to know how to find things in the ocean during World War I. Submarines could shoot torpedoes. They could sink ships.

Paul Langévin had an idea. He sent out a chirp. It was a fast sound like a ping. It would send back an echo if it bounced off something. Paul could see how long the echo took. He could figure out the distance. It wasn't ready in time to help during World War I. But when World War II came, the United States and British Navies were ready. The device is called SONAR. It stands for **SO**und **NA**vigation and **R**anging.

---

1 Paul Langévin recognized a problem. What is it?

_____

_____

_____

2 Paul Langévin took several important steps. What are two?

_____

_____

_____

3 What is the result of his steps?

_____

_____

_____

Name: _____ **Date:** _____

Ka-Boom!

Directions: Read the article. Then, answer the questions.

Star Spangled Banner

Rockets have been around for more than 1,000 years. First, they were used in China as toys mostly. People later started thinking about rockets differently. They could start fires. They were loud. So their next use was as a weapon. They were used in India to fight the British. So many were fired off at once that they scared the soldiers!

Sir William Congreve wanted to improve the rockets. He changed them so they could travel farther. His rockets were used by the British to fight the United States in 1812. They didn't do a lot of damage. But one big thing happened. Francis Scott Key was watching the battle. He saw the rockets. He saw the United States flag flying. And he wrote "The Star Spangled Banner."

1 How are rockets used first?

_____

_____

2 How are rockets used next?

_____

_____

3 How does Congreve improve the rockets?

_____

_____

4 What is the big result of using the rockets in the War of 1812?

_____

_____

Name: _____ **Date:** _____

A Hard-to-Hear Heartbeat

Directions: Read the article. Then, answer the questions.

The Stethoscope

René Laënnec had a problem. He was a young doctor in Paris in 1816. He needed to listen to a woman's heart and lungs. There wasn't such a thing as a stethoscope then. And the doctor wanted to be polite. He didn't want to lay his ear on her chest.

That is when he solved the problem, step by step. First, he remembered that you could put your ear on a piece of wood and hear a pin scratching at the other end. Second, he thought maybe he could hear sound from inside the chest in the same way. Third, he rolled up some paper and made a funnel. Last, he put the small end to his ear and the big end on her chest. Guess what! He could hear her heart and lungs!

1 What does René Laënnec do first to solve the problem?

_____

_____

2 What does he do second?

_____

_____

3 What does he do third?

_____

_____

4 What is the result of his steps?

_____

_____

Name: _____ **Date:** _____

A Coral Reef

Directions: Read the article. Then, answer the questions.

Coral

Have you ever held a piece of coral? It feels hard and stony. It was once very much alive. Tiny living animals live in the ocean. They gather together in **colonies**. Corals have **exoskeletons**. They protect their bodies. Corals deposit these exoskeletons. A coral reef can form where there are a lot of deposits. These places are a great place for fish to **reside**.

❶ In this article, the word **colonies** means

   a. animals that were once alive

   b. groups of animals

   c. skeletons of animals

❷ In this article, the word **exoskeletons** means

   a. protective parts of coral

   b. deposits of skeletons

   c. fish skeletons

❸ In this article, the word **reside** means

   a. live

   b. dive

   c. form

Name: _____ **Date:** _____

Glaciers!

Directions: Read the article. Then, answer the questions.

Glacier Watch

A glacier is a large body of ice. Glaciers **originate** on land where it is cold. The snow and sleet doesn't all melt away. The ice **accumulates** and it also moves across the land. While it moves, it **transports** rock and soil with it. Glaciers are made of fresh water, not seawater. Many people enjoy going to Alaska on cruise ships to see glaciers.

1 In this article, the word **originate** means

    a. move

    b. grow

    c. begin

2 In this article, the word **accumulates** means

    a. builds up

    b. flows

    c. melts

3 In this article, the word **transports** means

    a. thickens

    b. develops

    c. brings

Name: _____ **Date:** _____

Meaning Match

Directions: Draw a line to connect the word with the correct meaning. Use what you know about the root word and affixes to make your choices.

❶ adventurous   troublesome

❷ bothersome   not stopping

❸ circular   admirable

❹ continuous   feeling

❺ guardian   bold, daring

❻ honorable   in plain sight

❼ noticeable   protector

❽ probably   round

❾ sensibility   odd

❿ unusual   most likely

Name: _____ **Date:** _____

More Meaning Match

Directions: Draw a line to match the word with the correct meaning. Use what you know about the root word and affixes to make your choices.

1 announcement		hopeful
2 cowardice		sensible
3 expectant		sharpness
4 judgment		fearfulness
5 mastery		kindness
6 reasonable		message
7 scarcity		control
8 steepness		ruling
9 tenderness		honest
10 trustworthy		shortage

Name: _____ **Date:** _____

Root Detection

Directions: Circle the correct answer.

1 The root *erc* means press. You may know the word *exercise*.

The word *coerce* means

  a. to repeat

  b. to force

  c. to try

4 The root *fur* means rage. You may know the word *furious*.

The word *infuriate* means

  a. to make final

  b. to make weak

  c. to make mad

2 The root *dol* means pain or grief. You may know the word *condole*.

The word *doleful* means

  a. tired

  b. talkative

  c. sad

5 The root *horr* means dreadful. You may know the word *horror*.

The word *horrify* means

  a. appall or dismay

  b. consider or regard

  c. sadden or distress

3 The root *fer* means carry. You may know the word *transfer*.

The word *refer* means

  a. to pass on

  b. to take

  c. to reject

6 The root *un* means not. You may know the word *unnecessary*.

The word *uneven* means

  a. not even

  b. to add even numbers

  c. to make even

Name: _____ **Date:** _____

More Root Detection

Directions: Circle the correct answer.

1 The root *gress* means step or go. You may know the word *progress*.

The word *egress* means
- **a.** stopping point
- **b.** meeting place
- **c.** way out

2 The root *min* means small or less. You may know the word *minus*.

The word *minimize* means
- **a.** reduce
- **b.** refresh
- **c.** return

3 The root *lustr* means shine. You may know the word *illustrate*.

The word *lustrous* means
- **a.** lovely
- **b.** dull
- **c.** gleaming

4 The root *put* means think. You may know the word *compute*.

The word *dispute* means
- **a.** argue
- **b.** hate
- **c.** refuse

5 The root *ment* means mind. You may know the word *mental*.

The word *demented* means
- **a.** determined
- **b.** crazy
- **c.** furious

6 The root *ced* means go. You may know the word *recede*.

The word *proceed* means
- **a.** to pause
- **b.** to continue
- **c.** to stop

Name: _____ **Date:** _____

Dictionaries Rule!

Directions: Choose the best word for each sentence.

Dictionary Entries

enunciation—clearness of pronunciation

envious—wishing to have someone else's good fortune

environment—physical or social surroundings

envoy—messenger

epidemic—a rapidly spreading disease

epidermis—a thin outer layer of skin

epitaph—a brief statement on a tombstone

1 The little boy was _____ of his brother's new bike.

2 It is important to help keep the _____ clean.

3 The speaker had excellent _____.

4 Her _____ was simple: *Rest in Peace.*

5 There are germs on your body's _____.

6 The president was met by an _____.

7 Wash your hands often during a flu _____.

Name: _____ **Date:** _____

Glossaries Guide!

Directions: Choose the best word for each sentence.

Glossary Entries

electromagnet—a magnet with an electric coil wrapped around it, used to send waves of energy

generator—a machine that changes mechanical energy to electrical energy

phonograph—a device that plays recorded sound

radio broadcast—a program sent by radio waves

radio waves—electromagnetic waves used to send information

receiver—that part of a radio that receives the incoming signals or waves

---

1 The _____ needs more wire for the coil.

2 The first _____ was invented by Thomas Edison.

3 You can't see _____. But they are needed for radios to work.

4 A radio has to have a _____ to get the radio waves.

5 People were amazed to hear a human voice during the first _____.

6 Your electricity might go out in a storm. It is helpful to have a _____ that works with batteries.

Name: _____ **Date:** _____

Literal Meanings

There are many phrases that have a meaning that is different from the way the words are used. There are two meanings to these examples of using *a piece of cake*.

Example 1: I would like to eat *a piece of cake*.

Example 2: That test was *a piece of cake*.

Directions: Read the sentences. Rewrite each sentence to state its real meaning.

1 *He has a chip on his shoulder.* Let's avoid him.

_____

_____

2 I'm hungry. *Let's chow down.*

_____

_____

3 Look at the time. *She is racing against the clock.*

_____

_____

4 It's 8:00. *It's time to hit the sack.*

_____

_____

5 Let me do it. *I know the ropes.*

_____

_____

Name: _____ **Date:** _____

More Literal Meanings

There are many phrases that have a meaning that is different from the way the words are used. There are two meanings to these examples of using *over the top*.

Example 1: Put the cover *over the top* of the chair.

Example 2: The queen's gown was *over the top*.

Directions: Read the sentences. Rewrite each sentence to state its real meaning.

1 *The girl was the apple of his eye.* She couldn't do anything wrong.

_____

_____

2 *Hold your horses.* Let me answer.

_____

_____

3 I didn't do it. *You're barking up the wrong tree.*

_____

_____

4 Don't feel bad. *We're all in the same boat.*

_____

_____

5 The food is here! *Let's pig out!*

_____

_____

Name: _____ **Date:** _____

Word Connections

Directions: Different words go with different professions. Sort the words into the correct profession.

Word Bank

allergies	appetizer	assignment	bacteria	bake
bandage	boil	broil	checkup	classroom
cook	cough	course	disease	dropout
first aid	fruit	fry	grade	herb
homework	instruction	medicine	painkillers	principal
recipe	school	spice	subject	wound

Chef's list	Teacher's list	Doctor's list

Name: _____ **Date:** _____

More Word Connections

Directions: Different words go with each of the five senses. Sort the words into the appropriate category.

Word Bank

acrid	bitter	bumpy	brilliant	buzz	cold	uneven
crunch	delicious	echo	fragrant	juicy	musty	hazy
prickly	purr	reddish	shadowy	slimy	smoky	strong
sweet	tart	ugly	whimper			

Sight words	Touch words	Hearing words

Smell words	Taste words

Name: _____ Date: _____

Meaning Match!

Directions: Find a synonym for each word. *Hint:* All the words can be used as adjectives.

Word Bank

abrupt	brave	dangerous	delicate
effective	fascinating	grateful	glum
persistent	reckless	shy	timeless

1 courageous _____

2 careless _____

3 thankful _____

4 enchanting _____

5 timid _____

6 eternal _____

7 successful _____

8 hazardous _____

9 sudden _____

10 breakable _____

11 sad _____

12 constant _____

Name: _____ **Date:** _____

More Meaning Match!

Directions: Find a synonym for each word.   *Hint*: All the words can be used as nouns.

Word Bank

base   celebration   diner   cottage   hermit   peak

pure   refuge   rubbish   suitcases   thief   wealth

1 luggage _____

2 riches _____

3 crook _____

4 loner _____

5 bungalow _____

6 festivity _____

7 café _____

8 foundation _____

9 trash _____

10 clean _____

11 retreat _____

12 top _____

Name: _____ **Date:** _____

It's About Time!

Directions: Choose the best word.

Word Bank

after	always	before	early	late
later	never	rarely	soon	usually

1 I play football once in a while. I play _____.

2 I can't wait for dinner. I want it to come _____.

3 I missed my bus. I got to the bus stop too _____.

4 I will set my alarm clock. I need to get up _____ tomorrow.

5 I _____ eat dessert. I love it!

6 I can't eat my dessert until _____ I eat my vegetables.

7 My cat _____ eats dog food. He hates it.

8 I _____ walk to school but today I will ride my bike.

9 Mom reads me a story _____ I go to sleep.

10 The sun comes up _____ in the winter.

Name: _____ **Date:** _____

It's About Position!

A **preposition** is a word that shows a connection.

Example 1: The cat is *in* the box.

Example 2: The box is *by* the table.

Example 3: Be sure he doesn't jump *onto* the table.

In these examples, the prepositions all show position.

Directions: Underline the preposition in each sentence. *Hint*: Some sentences have more than one preposition.

1 Most people travel by driving in their cars.

2 But some people travel under the ground.

3 Those people often have to walk down the stairs.

4 Then they get on a platform.

5 When the subway arrives, they have to get inside the car quickly.

6 When they arrive at the station, they get out of the subway.

7 They probably have to go up the stairs or escalator.

8 They may have to walk along a hallway to catch another subway.

9 The first subway was built in London.

10 Take a subway the next time you go to a big city. It's fun!

Name: _____ **Date:** _____

Clang! Clang!

Directions: Read the text. Then, answer the questions.

Cable Cars

San Francisco has steep hills. One day, Andrew Smith Hallidie saw what could happen on those hills. The year was 1869. Streets were made of bumpy cobblestones. It rains a lot there in the winter. That makes for slippery streets. On that wet day, Mr. Hallidie watched some horses try to pull a heavy load up a hill. The horses were whipped. They fell and were dragged to their deaths.

Mr. Hallidie's father had invented a wire rope. Hallidie had used this cable to haul up ore when mining. He decided to use what he knew to build a cable system that would pull cars up steep hills. There are plenty of strong machines to get things up steep hills today. But you can still take a cable car in San Francisco.

---

1 How do people get loads up hills in San Francisco?

   a. They push them up.

   b. They use horses.

   c. They use cable cars.

2 List three things that contribute to the problem Mr. Hallidie saw.

_____

_____

_____

3 Why do you think San Francisco still has cable cars?

_____

_____

Name: _____ **Date:** _____

Earthquake!

Directions: Read the text. Then, answer the questions.

Moving Ground

Have you ever wondered why there are earthquakes? The earth has a crust made of big sheets of rock. Some of these plates are next to each other. Some overlap. Underneath the crust is a lot of hot liquid and more rocks. Just like you, the liquid is always moving. Sometimes, like a boiling teakettle, the pressure builds up.

All the pressure has to go somewhere! There is a big shift underground. Think of it as the earth giving itself a shake to relieve the pressure. It could be like a quick snap. It could be a wave-like movement that flows up through the earth, getting wider as it comes. Your bed might sway back and forth for a few seconds. Books might fall off your shelf. A few earthquakes are dangerous. But they are rare. Most just last a few seconds.

1 Why does the earth shift underground?

   a. There is a shake and a snap.

   b. There is pressure that has built up.

   c. There is a wave of movement that goes up.

2 Write two things that might happen during an earthquake.

_____

_____

3 Think about the opinion of the writer. Should you worry about earthquakes? Why or why not?

_____

_____

_____

_____

Name: _____ **Date:** _____

Dangerous Waves!

Directions: Read the text. Then, answer the questions.

Tsunami

A tsunami is a set of ocean waves caused by a sudden disruption of the sea's surface. There are several causes for this. There might be an earthquake. There could be a volcano that explodes. Most often, a tsunami is caused by a large earthquake in or near the ocean. The "waves" of the earthquake move the sea, too. The waves in the sea then move, too. They pick up speed as they travel. They also get higher.

An earthquake in Japan caused a major tsunami in 2011. The earthquake was huge. It destroyed many buildings. Less than 30 minutes later the tsunami began. Waves built to more than 100 feet high. Thousands of people were killed. Many lost everything they owned. Many tsunamis disappear as they move through the ocean. But when they don't, it can be devastating.

1 List three causes for a tsunami.

_____

_____

_____

2 What causes a tsunami?

_____

_____

_____

3 List two results of the tsunami in Japan.

_____

_____

Name: _____ **Date:** _____

The Olympics

Directions: Read the text. Then, answer the questions.

Sporting Games

The Olympics began many years ago in ancient Greece. The games were held to honor the Greek gods of war. There are several ways that those Olympics are like ours today. Just like now, they were held every four years. They had music. They had special displays. Instead of many different competitions, however, there was one race. It was 200 yards long.

More games were added over the years. The Greeks raced chariots. They wrestled and threw spears. Discus throwing and jumping events were held. Just like today, the games took a lot of preparation. But during ancient times, there was one very tough game. It was called the *pankration*. The contestants could fight any way they wanted. And they fought until they gave up—or died!

1 List three ways that the ancient Olympics are like today's games.

_____

_____

_____

2 List two ways in which the games are different.

_____

_____

3 Describe the *pankration*.

_____

_____

_____

_____

Name: _____ **Date:** _____

Fables

Directions: A moral is the lesson taught by a fable. Read the story.
Then, answer the questions.

The Snake and the Eagle

An eagle flew down and caught a snake. The eagle wanted to
eat the snake. But the snake wrapped around him and began to
squeeze. They fought fiercely. A farmer saw the struggle. He rushed
up and pulled the eagle free from the snake.
As the snake slithered off, it saw the man's jug
of water. He spat his poison in the jug. As the
man started to leave, the eagle saw that the
man was about to take a drink. He flew over
and knocked the jug to the ground.

❶ What good thing did the man do?

_____

_____

_____

❷ What good thing did the eagle do?

_____

_____

_____

❸ What is the moral of the story?

   a. One good act deserves another.

   b. It is useless attacking the foolish.

   c. What is most valuable is often not recognized.

Name: _____ **Date:** _____

Fable Message

Directions: A moral is the lesson taught by a fable. Read the story.
Then, answer the questions.

The Stag at the Pool

A stag stopped at a pool to drink. He saw his reflection in the pool.
"Look at my beautiful antlers! If only I had big legs and feet like my
antlers! I would be even more handsome!" While he was admiring
himself, a lion sneaked up. The stag began
to run, speeding over the smooth plain. He
managed to stay ahead of the lion. Then he
came to the woods. He could not move so
quickly through the dense forest. His antlers
got in the way. Soon the lion caught him. Soon
the stag regretted his thoughts at the pool.

1 What mistake did does stag make?

_____

_____

_____

2 What is the moral of the story?

   a. Appearances can be deceiving.

   b. Do not believe everything you see.

   c. You should appreciate what you have.

Name: _____ **Date:** _____

Another Fable Message

Directions: A moral is the lesson taught by a fable. Read the story. Then, answer the questions.

The Town Mouse and the Country Mouse

A town mouse decided to visit his cousin in the country. The country mouse had a simple life. He fed his town cousin beans, bacon, cheese, and a bit of bread. The town mouse didn't understand how a mouse could get by on such plain food. "You should come and live with me," the town mouse said. "In my home, there is grand food from a grand table." The country mouse came to visit. Indeed, there were wonderful foods left on the table. As the country mouse

ate some cake, he saw a huge cat leaping across the table. "Run!" the town mouse said. They ran behind the wall where the town mouse lived. The country mouse packed his things. "What is the problem?" the town mouse asked. "You just have to be quick. That cat will never catch you." The country mouse replied, "No thanks!"

---

❶ How are the mice different?

_____

_____

_____

❷ What is the moral of the story?

a. You can't trust some friends even if you like them.

b. It's better to eat beans and bacon in peace than cake in fear.

c. It's better to live in the city than in the country.

Name: _____ **Date:** _____

More Fables

. . . .

Directions: A moral is the lesson taught by a fable. Read the story. Then, answer the questions.

The Wolf and the Goat

A wolf saw a goat feeding high on the side of a mountain. The wolf was very hungry. But he had no way of reaching the goat. "Come lower, my friend," called the wolf. "You might fall off that cliff. Besides, the grass in the meadow is tall. There is so much more to eat." The goat was very wise. She knew what the wolf wanted.

❶ What do you think the goat said to the wolf?

_____

_____

_____

❷ What is the moral of the story?

   a. Beware of a friend that has other plans for you.

   b. Beware of a friend that says you might fall off a cliff.

   c. Beware of a friend that is not smart.

Name: _____ **Date:** _____

What Does It Really Mean?

Directions: Idioms are phrases or sentences that have a different meaning from the words. Match the idioms with their meanings.

1 A bird in the hand is worth two in the bush.

2 A leopard can't change his spots.

3 Those are a dime a dozen.

4 They must cost an arm and a leg.

5 Every cloud has a silver lining.

6 Curiosity killed the cat.

7 They'd bend over backwards for me.

8 Get down to brass tacks.

They are easy to get or inexpensive.

They are very expensive.

They are willing to help.

Time to be serious.

It's better to have something that is certain than taking a risk for more.

You can't change who you are.

Even tough times have something good about them.

Don't go where you shouldn't.

Name: _____ **Date:** _____

More Sayings to Learn

Directions: Idioms are phrases or sentences that have a different meaning from the words. Match the idioms with their meanings.

1 A penny saved is a penny earned.

2 Don't put all your eggs in one basket.

3 Bite your tongue!

4 Don't add fuel to the fire.

5 Don't count your chickens before they are hatched.

6 We're all in the same boat.

7 It's in the bag.

8 Go out on a limb.

Don't rely on something unknown.

Everyone is dealing with the same problem.

Take a risk.

It's worth saving everything you can.

It's definitely going to happen.

Don't talk.

Don't make things worse.

Don't limit your options.

Name: _____ **Date:** _____

The Written Word

Directions: Read the definitions for different parts of a play. Choose the best word for each sentence.

> **act**—a major part of a play
>
> **play**—a literary work that is performed on a stage
>
> **scene**—a portion of an act in which the setting is fixed
>
> **script**—written text of a play

1 The students put on a _____ called *Dragon Trouble.*

2 Each actor got a copy of the _____ to study.

3 The first _____ had two scenes.

4 Each _____ had its own background.

Directions: Read the definitions for different parts of a book or poem. Choose the best word for each sentence.

> **chapter**—section of a book
>
> **glossary**—an alphabetical list of words related to a subject
>
> **index**—alphabetical list of names, places, and subjects and their page numbers in a book
>
> **stanza**—a part of a poem or song, a verse

5 Our teacher said we should read one _____ of the book each night.

6 The students each read aloud a _____ of the poem.

7 The _____ or _____ can be found at the end of some books.

Name: _____ **Date:** _____

Mood Match

Directions: Look at the pictures. Each shows a mood. Choose a word that matches each picture.

Word Bank

anger   fear   joy   kindness   loneliness   playfulness

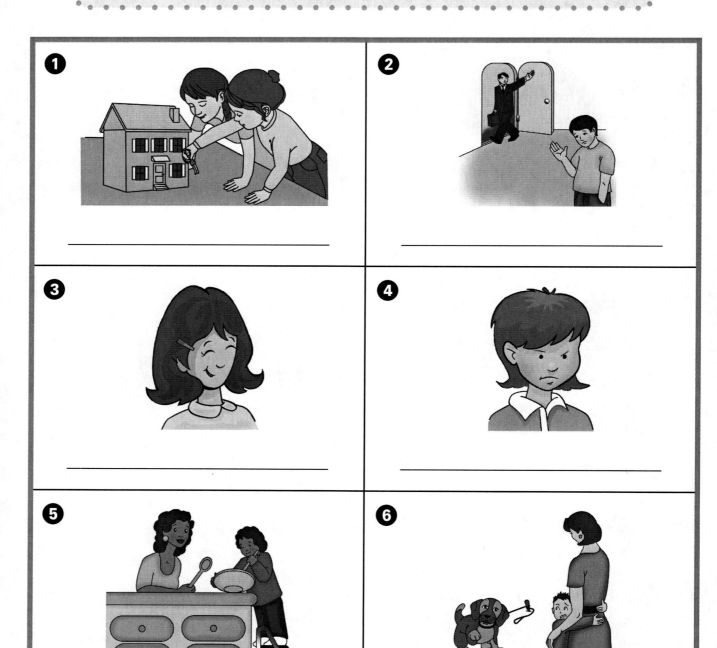

1 _____

2 _____

3 _____

4 _____

5 _____

6 _____

Name: _____ **Date:** _____

Comparison Chart

Directions: To compare stories, it can be useful to fill out a chart. The next time you read two stories or books by the same author, fill out this chart.

Author's Name _____

Book Title _____	Book Title _____
Type of Story _____	Type of Story _____
Setting _____ _____	Setting _____ _____
Main Character _____	Main Character _____
Minor Character _____	Minor Character _____
Problem _____ _____ _____	Problem _____ _____ _____
Ending _____ _____ _____	Ending _____ _____ _____
Rating (1 to 5) _____	Rating (1 to 5) _____

Name: _____ **Date:** _____

Compare Characters

Directions: To compare characters, it can be helpful to fill out a chart. The next time you read a book with strong characters, fill out the chart below.

Comparing Characters	Character's Name _____	Character's Name _____
What does the character look like?		
What problem does the character face?		
What steps does the character take?		
What kinds of success does the character have?		
What kinds of failures does the character have?		
How does the character resolve the problem?		
Would you want to meet this character? Why or why not?		

Once Is Not Enough For Reading!

Directions: Try one or more of these ideas below to practice being a better reader.

- Don't be afraid to substitute a word if you are reading aloud. It's okay, as long as it makes sense. You can check the word later (and you might be right).

- Read in a famous person's voice, such as a movie or television star.

- Read to a family member in a cartoon character's voice.

- Read in fun voices, such as how you think your dog or cat would talk.

- Read and record the book. Play it for someone in your family.

- Read in a silly voice.

- Watch a movie version of the book. Then, make your own movie script.

- Choose music that goes with the movie version. Read your script with the music.

- Create an award as if you won a major award. Read aloud your acceptance speech.

Read It Again—And Have Fun!

Directions: Find a partner. Then, try one or more of these ideas below to practice being a better reader.

- Read one page aloud. Have a friend read the next page.

- Choose characters. Read in the characters' voices.

- Read the characters in the opposite way that they should sound.

- Read the book aloud as a duet, with one high and one low voice.

- Read poetry, trading verses.

- Have a good reader read part of the book. Then, read it the same way.

- Read the book as if you were superheroes.

- Take turns making up new endings. Surprise each other.

- Read in opposites. One reads high, one low. One reads fast, one slow.

- Be television reporters and read the book aloud.

Name: _____ **Date:** _____

A Real Hero

Directions: When writing your opinion, it helps to organize your thoughts. Choose a real person or fictional character that you believe is a hero. Complete this form by writing the evidence to support the statements.

Evidence	
My choice for a real hero is _____.	
The person takes action.	_____ _____
The person is thoughtful.	_____ _____
The person makes good choices.	_____ _____
The person keeps trying.	_____ _____
The person makes a sacrifice.	_____ _____
The person is loyal.	_____ _____
The person is brave.	_____ _____
The person is focused.	_____ _____

Name: _____ **Date:** _____

Can You Explain That?

Directions: If you were a soldier in the Civil War, you might need to make hardtack. The ingredients are listed. The equipment shows some clues about what to do. Try to explain the steps for making it.

Ingredients for twelve 3" squares	Equipment
3 cups flour	1 bowl
2 teaspoons salt	1 spoon
1 cup water	a place to roll out the dough
	1 rolling pin
	1 knife for cutting the dough
	1 nail for poking holes in the dough
	1 pan for baking
	1 oven heated to 375°F

_____

_____

_____

_____

_____

_____

_____

_____

_____

Name: _____ **Date:** _____

Cause and Effect

Directions: Try using this form to help you write an article that uses cause and effect.

Word Bank

Because of	The reasons for	Another reason
As a result of	Then	So
Therefore	Finally	In conclusion

Write an introductory sentence.

_____

_____

What was the event or action that started the change?

_____

_____

Write the second sentence or cause.

_____

_____

Write what happened as a result.

_____

_____

_____

_____

Write an ending sentence.

_____

_____

_____

_____

Name: _____ **Date:** _____

Have a Great Trip!

Directions: Write a story on a separate sheet of paper about a character that goes on a journey. Use the chart to help you organize the story.

Main character	
Main character's goal	
Setting	
Villain	
Villain's goal	
Problems and challenges	
Actions of characters	
Outcomes of actions	
Ending	

Quick Writes

Directions: Try the ideas listed below to practice becoming a good writer.

- Postcards from a journey

- Emails between your imaginary friends

- Emails between two characters

- Movie reviews

- Bumper stickers

- A shopping list for a favorite book character

- Voicemails between your pets

- A complaint to a book character

- A description of your favorite restaurant

- A description of your favorite amusement park

- A description of your favorite vacation spot

- A horoscope or fortune for your grandparents

- A poem about your favorite stuffed animal

- A story written by your favorite stuffed animal

- A diary entry from your favorite stuffed animal

More Quick Writes

Directions: Try the ideas listed below to practice becoming a good writer.

- Wanted ad for the perfect brother or sister

- A letter to the man on the moon

- A letter to your favorite relative

- A description of your dream playroom

- A saying for a T-shirt

- A saying for a button

- A menu for a comic character

- Scrapbook pages for a favorite character

- The life story of a rock

- The life story of a reptile

- An acceptance speech for your sports trophy

- An acceptance speech for your film award

- An acceptance speech for your singing award

- A list of hated foods

- What you'd do with $100.00

#50886—Bright & Brainy: 3rd Grade Practice © *Shell Education*

Name: _____ **Date:** _____

Research

Directions: Writing short research reports takes organization. Use this sheet to help you get started.

Topic _____

Write what you already know about the topic.

_____

_____

_____

_____

_____

Write some questions about the topic.

_____

_____

_____

_____

_____

List possible sources for the research.

_____

_____

_____

_____

_____

Research *(cont.)*

Directions: Writing short research reports takes organization. Use this sheet to help you collect information.

Topic _____

Name of source _____

Date of source _____

Author of source _____

Publisher of source _____

Information from source _____

_____

_____

_____

_____

Topic _____

Name of source _____

Date of source _____

Author of source _____

Publisher of source _____

Information from source _____

_____

_____

_____

Speak Up!

Directions: Find a partner to read a book with. Cut out the questions from this list. Put them in a bag and take turns answering the questions.

How does the title relate to the story?

What surprised you? Why?

Choose a character and explain how you are alike or different from the character.

Who should or should not read this book? Why?

Which character would you like to have as a friend? Why?

What minor character would you like to get to know better? Why?

What was the main challenge or problem in the book?

What emotions did the book cause you to feel?

What was the best and worst part about the ending?

What do you think will happen after the ending?

If you were the author, what would you have done differently?

What should the author write about next? Why?

This page is intentionally blank.

Listen Up!

Directions: Play these games to practice being a good speaker and listener.

Secret Word

This game is for at least three people. Select a speaker and whisper a secret word to him or her. The speaker has to give a one-minute speech using the word no more than three times. The listeners have to guess what the secret word is.

Spelling Word Fun

This game is for two or more players. Select a leader and write 20 spelling words on 3" × 5" index cards. Place them right side up on a table, spread out and mixed up. The leader softly calls out a word. The remaining players try to find the word. The first one to get the card keeps it. The player with the most cards after ten turns becomes the new leader.

Adverb Fun

This game is for at least three players. One player is sent out of the room. The group or leader thinks of an adverb. The player returns and asks questions of other players. They can be any sort of question, such as "Where do you live? Where were you born?" The answering player responds in the style of the adverb. The questioning player has to guess the adverb.

Name: _____ **Date:** _____

Number Round-Up!

Here's how to round numbers:

- If the number ends in 1 through 4, round it to the next lower number that ends in 0.

- If the number ends in 5 through 9, round it to the next higher number that ends in 0.

Directions: Round the numbers to the nearest 10.

1 33 rounds to _____

2 72 rounds to _____

3 37 rounds to _____

4 42 rounds to _____

5 82 rounds to _____

6 61 rounds to _____

7 77 rounds to _____

8 7 rounds to _____

9 15 rounds to _____

10 29 rounds to _____

11 66 rounds to _____

12 12 rounds to _____

13 49 rounds to _____

14 21 rounds to _____

15 5 rounds to _____

16 92 rounds to _____

17 17 rounds to _____

18 22 rounds to _____

19 94 rounds to _____

20 47 rounds to _____

Name: _____ **Date:** _____

More Tens Round-Up!

Here's how to round numbers:

- If the number ends in 1 through 4, round it to the next lower number that ends in 0.

- If the number ends in 5 through 9, round it to the next higher number that ends in 0.

Directions: Round the numbers to the nearest 10.

1 48 rounds to _____   **2** 76 rounds to _____

3 27 rounds to _____   **4** 72 rounds to _____

5 87 rounds to _____   **6** 91 rounds to _____

7 72 rounds to _____   **8** 18 rounds to _____

9 18 rounds to _____   **10** 9 rounds to _____

11 69 rounds to _____   **12** 93 rounds to _____

13 45 rounds to _____   **14** 27 rounds to _____

15 15 rounds to _____   **16** 73 rounds to _____

17 14 rounds to _____   **18** 21 rounds to _____

19 54 rounds to _____   **20** 56 rounds to _____

Name: _____ **Date:** _____

Big Number Round-Up!

Here's how to round numbers:

- If the number ends in 1 through 4, round it to the next lower number that ends in 0.

- If the number ends in 5 through 9, round it to the next higher number that ends in 0.

Directions: Round the numbers to the nearest 10.

1 133 rounds to _____

2 173 rounds to _____

3 812 rounds to _____

4 166 rounds to _____

5 511 rounds to _____

6 388 rounds to _____

7 229 rounds to _____

8 99 rounds to _____

9 442 rounds to _____

10 994 rounds to _____

11 676 rounds to _____

12 425 rounds to _____

13 681 rounds to _____

14 726 rounds to _____

15 259 rounds to _____

16 192 rounds to _____

17 261 rounds to _____

18 912 rounds to _____

19 98 rounds to _____

20 347 rounds to _____

Name: _____ **Date:** _____

More Big Number Round-Up!

Here's how to round numbers:

- If the number ends in 1 through 4, round it to the next lower number that ends in 0.

- If the number ends in 5 through 9, round it to the next higher number that ends in 0.

Directions: Round the numbers to the nearest 10.

1 418 rounds to _____   **2** 237 rounds to _____

3 873 rounds to _____   **4** 724 rounds to _____

5 187 rounds to _____   **6** 698 rounds to _____

7 495 rounds to _____   **8** 915 rounds to _____

9 142 rounds to _____   **10** 555 rounds to _____

11 762 rounds to _____   **12** 472 rounds to _____

13 991 rounds to _____   **14** 189 rounds to _____

15 97 rounds to _____   **16** 193 rounds to _____

17 237 rounds to _____   **18** 713 rounds to _____

19 231 rounds to _____   **20** 566 rounds to _____

Name: _____ Date: _____

Add Big Numbers!

One way of adding big numbers is to expand the numbers.

Example: $400 + 20 + 9 = 429$

        $+ \; 300 + 30 + 5 = 335$

        $700 + 50 + 14 = 764$

Directions: Add the numbers by expanding them.

1

$200 + 50 + 4 = 254$

$+ \; 700 + 20 + 7 = 727$

$900 + 70 + 11 = 981$

2

_____ + _____ + _____ = 369

_____ + _____ + _____ = 514

_____ + _____ + _____ =

3

_____ + _____ + _____ = 555

_____ + _____ + _____ = 217

_____ + _____ + _____ =

4

_____ + _____ + _____ = 174

_____ + _____ + _____ = 843

_____ + _____ + _____ =

5

_____ + _____ + _____ = 162

_____ + _____ + _____ = 852

_____ + _____ + _____ =

6

_____ + _____ + _____ = 234

_____ + _____ + _____ = 156

_____ + _____ + _____ =

Name: _____ **Date:** _____

Add More Big Numbers!

It's easy to add big numbers. Just start at the right. Add the ones first, then the tens, and finally the hundreds.

$$
\begin{array}{r}
1 \\
116 \\
+\ 127 \\
\hline
243
\end{array}
$$

Directions: Solve the problems. Regroup as needed.

1 $\begin{array}{r}817 \\ +\ 108 \\ \hline\end{array}$	**2** $\begin{array}{r}245 \\ +\ 347 \\ \hline\end{array}$
3 $\begin{array}{r}529 \\ +\ 252 \\ \hline\end{array}$	**4** $\begin{array}{r}179 \\ +\ 109 \\ \hline\end{array}$
5 $\begin{array}{r}606 \\ +\ 126 \\ \hline\end{array}$	**6** $\begin{array}{r}333 \\ +\ 557 \\ \hline\end{array}$
7 $\begin{array}{r}832 \\ +\ 158 \\ \hline\end{array}$	**8** $\begin{array}{r}909 \\ +\ \ 89 \\ \hline\end{array}$

Name: _____ **Date:** _____

Add Even More Big Numbers!

It's easy to add big numbers. Add the ones first, then the tens, and finally the hundreds.

$$\begin{array}{r} {}^{1}{}^{1}367 \\ +\ 457 \\ \hline 824 \end{array}$$

Directions: Solve the problems. Regroup as needed.

❶ $\begin{array}{r} 325 \\ +\ 197 \\ \hline \end{array}$	❷ $\begin{array}{r} 391 \\ +\ 259 \\ \hline \end{array}$	❸ $\begin{array}{r} 119 \\ +\ 149 \\ \hline \end{array}$
❹ $\begin{array}{r} 725 \\ +\ 177 \\ \hline \end{array}$	❺ $\begin{array}{r} 666 \\ +\ 266 \\ \hline \end{array}$	❻ $\begin{array}{r} 88 \\ +\ 122 \\ \hline \end{array}$
❼ $\begin{array}{r} 189 \\ +\ 289 \\ \hline \end{array}$	❽ $\begin{array}{r} 455 \\ +\ 455 \\ \hline \end{array}$	❾ $\begin{array}{r} 788 \\ +\ 122 \\ \hline \end{array}$

Name: _____ **Date:** _____

Subtract Big Numbers!

One way of subtracting big numbers is to expand the numbers.

Example:

$$
\begin{array}{r}
400 + 30 + 9 = 439 \\
- \ \ 300 + 20 + 5 = 325 \\
\hline
100 + 10 + 4 = 114
\end{array}
$$

Directions: Subtract the numbers by expanding them.

1 $\begin{array}{r} 700 + 20 + 7 = 727 \\ -\ 200 + 10 + 4 = 214 \\ \hline 500 + 10 + 3 = 513 \end{array}$	**2** $\begin{array}{r} +\ \ + \ \ = 598 \\ -\ +\ \ +\ \ = 514 \\ \hline +\ \ +\ \ = \end{array}$
3 $\begin{array}{r} +\ \ +\ \ = 448 \\ -\ +\ \ +\ \ = 217 \\ \hline +\ \ +\ \ = \end{array}$	**4** $\begin{array}{r} +\ \ +\ \ = 474 \\ -\ +\ \ +\ \ = 241 \\ \hline +\ \ +\ \ = \end{array}$
5 $\begin{array}{r} +\ \ +\ \ = 962 \\ -\ +\ \ +\ \ = 752 \\ \hline +\ \ +\ \ = \end{array}$	**6** $\begin{array}{r} +\ \ +\ \ = 999 \\ -\ +\ \ +\ \ = 756 \\ \hline +\ \ +\ \ = \end{array}$
7 $\begin{array}{r} +\ \ +\ \ = 880 \\ -\ +\ \ +\ \ = 160 \\ \hline +\ \ +\ \ = \end{array}$	**8** $\begin{array}{r} +\ \ +\ \ = 666 \\ -\ +\ \ +\ \ = 333 \\ \hline +\ \ +\ \ = \end{array}$

Name: _____ **Date:** _____

Subtract More Big Numbers!

Subtracting with regrouping takes several steps.

- First subtract the ones. The number 8 is larger than 7, so you need to use ten from the tens column.

- Change the 6 to a 5 to show that one of the tens is joining with the 7 to make 17. Subtract 8 from 17 in the ones column.

- Then, subtract 4 from 5 in the tens column. The last step is to subtract the numbers in the hundreds column.

$$\begin{array}{r} \overset{5\ 17}{5\cancel{6}7} \\ -\ 248 \\ \hline 319 \end{array}$$

Directions: Subtract the problems.

❶

$$\begin{array}{r} 983 \\ -\ 746 \\ \hline \end{array}$$

❷

$$\begin{array}{r} 662 \\ -\ 217 \\ \hline \end{array}$$

❸

$$\begin{array}{r} 427 \\ -\ 318 \\ \hline \end{array}$$

❹

$$\begin{array}{r} 526 \\ -\ 308 \\ \hline \end{array}$$

❺

$$\begin{array}{r} 837 \\ -\ 109 \\ \hline \end{array}$$

❻

$$\begin{array}{r} 491 \\ -\ 333 \\ \hline \end{array}$$

#50886—Bright & Brainy: 3rd Grade Practice

Name: _____ **Date:** _____

Subtract Even More Big Numbers!

Directions: Subtract the problems.

1
```
  534
- 148
```

2
```
  227
- 138
```

3
```
  525
- 256
```

4
```
  253
- 158
```

5
```
  493
- 394
```

6
```
  488
- 479
```

7
```
  770
- 586
```

8
```
  555
- 466
```

9
```
  639
- 369
```

Name: _____ **Date:** _____

It's All About Tens!

The chart below is organized by sets of tens. The first column has 1 set of 10, which equals 10 dots. The next column has 2 sets of 10. You can figure out how many that is by using addition or multiplication.

You can use addition:

$$\begin{array}{r} 10 \\ + 10 \\ \hline 20 \end{array}$$

You can use multiplication:

$$\begin{array}{r} 10 \\ \times\ 2 \\ \hline 20 \end{array}$$

Directions: Finish the chart.

1	2	3	4	5	6	7	8	9	10
:::::	:::::	:::::	:::::	:::::	:::::	:::::	:::::	:::::	:::::
	:::::	:::::	:::::	:::::	:::::	:::::	:::::	:::::	:::::
		:::::	:::::	:::::	:::::	:::::	:::::	:::::	:::::
			:::::	:::::	:::::	:::::	:::::	:::::	:::::
				:::::	:::::	:::::	:::::	:::::	:::::
					:::::	:::::	:::::	:::::	:::::
						:::::	:::::	:::::	:::::
							:::::	:::::	:::::
								:::::	:::::
									:::::
10 dots	**20 dots**	____ dots	____ dots	____ dots	____ dots	____ dots	____ dots	____ dots	____ dots

Name: _____ **Date:** _____

Multiply Those Tens!

Directions: Practice multiplying by 10.

1 2 × 10 = _____

2 10 × 6 = _____

3 7 × 10 = _____

4 10 × 1 = _____

5 1 × 10 = _____

6 10 × 4 = _____

7 4 × 10 = _____

8 10 × 2 = _____

9 3 × 10 = _____

10 10 × 3 = _____

11 6 × 10 = _____

12 10 × 5 = _____

13 8 × 10 = _____

14 10 × 8 = _____

15 5 × 10 = _____

16 10 × 7 = _____

17 9 × 10 = _____

18 10 × 9 = _____

19 10 × 10 = _____

20 10 × 0 = _____

Name: _____ **Date:** _____

Multiply More Tens!

Directions: Practice multiplying by 10.

1 $2 \times$ _____ $= 20$	**2** _____ $\times 10 = 70$
3 _____ $\times 10 = 40$	**4** _____ $\times 10 = 60$
5 _____ $\times 10 = 10$	**6** _____ $\times 10 = 80$
7 _____ $\times 10 = 50$	**8** _____ $\times 10 = 90$
9 _____ $\times 10 = 30$	**10** _____ $\times 10 = 0$
11 $10 \times$ _____ $= 40$	**12** $10 \times$ _____ $= 60$
13 $10 \times$ _____ $= 80$	**14** $10 \times$ _____ $= 90$
15 $10 \times$ _____ $= 0$	**16** $10 \times$ _____ $= 70$
17 $10 \times$ _____ $= 20$	**18** $10 \times$ _____ $= 10$
19 $10 \times$ _____ $= 50$	**20** $10 \times$ _____ $= 30$

#50886—Bright & Brainy: 3rd Grade Practice

Name: _____ **Date:** _____

Find the Number!

How many groups of 4 sticks do you see?

How many sticks are there in total?

You can write the problem like this:

8 groups of 4 sticks = 32 sticks or 8 × 4 = 32

Directions: Solve the problems.

❶ 6 groups of 4 sticks = _____ sticks

❷ 4 groups of 4 sticks = _____ sticks

❸ 2 groups of 4 sticks = _____ sticks

❹ 5 groups of 4 sticks = _____ sticks

❺ 1 group of 4 sticks = _____ sticks

❻ 8 groups of 4 sticks = _____ sticks

❼ 3 groups of 4 sticks = _____ sticks

❽ 7 groups of 4 sticks = _____ sticks

Directions: Use the sticks to compute these answers.

❾ 4 groups of 4 sticks is the same as saying: 4 × 4 = _____

❿ 3 groups of 4 sticks is the same as saying: 3 × 4 = _____

⓫ 9 groups of 4 sticks is the same as saying: 9 × 4 = _____

⓬ 5 groups of 4 sticks is the same as saying: 5 × 4 = _____

Name: _____ Date: _____

Find More Numbers!

How many groups of 3 dots do you see?

How many dots are there in total?

You can write the problem like this:

10 groups of 3 dots = 30 dots or 10 × 3 = 30

Directions: Solve the problems.

1 9 groups of 3 dots = _____ dots

2 4 groups of 3 dots = _____ dots

3 8 groups of 3 dots = _____ dots

4 2 groups of 3 dots = _____ dots

5 5 groups of 3 dots = _____ dots

6 1 group of 3 dots = _____ dots

7 6 group of 3 dots = _____ dots

8 10 group of 3 dots = _____ dots

Directions: Use the dots to compute these answers.

9 9 groups of 3 dots is the same as saying: 9 × 3 = _____

10 3 groups of 3 dots is the same as saying: 3 × 3 = _____

11 7 groups of 3 dots is the same as saying: 7 × 3 = _____

12 1 group of 3 dots is the same as saying: 1 × 3 = _____

Name: _____ **Date:** _____

Multiplication Basics

A multiplication chart can be used to find any problem. To find the answer to a problem, such as 4 times 8, run one finger down the 4 column. Run another finger across the 8 row. They meet at the number 32.

$$4 \times 8 = 32$$

×	1	2	3	4	5	6	7	8	9	10	11	12
1	1	2	3	4	5	6	7	8	9	10	11	12
2	2	4	6	8	10	12	14	16	18	20	22	24
3	3	6	9	12	15	18	21	24	27	30	33	36
4	4	8	12	16	20	24	28	32	36	40	44	48
5	5	10	15	20	25	30	35	40	45	50	55	60
6	6	12	18	24	30	36	42	48	54	60	66	72
7	7	14	21	28	35	42	49	56	63	70	77	84
8	8	16	24	32	40	48	56	64	72	80	88	96
9	9	18	27	36	45	54	63	72	81	90	99	108
10	10	20	30	40	50	60	70	80	90	100	110	120
11	11	22	33	44	55	66	77	88	99	110	121	132
12	12	24	36	48	60	72	84	96	108	120	132	144

Name: _____ **Date:** _____

Sticky Groups!

Many numbers can be divided into equal amounts.

 For example, this group of sticks has been sorted into 3 groups of 10 sticks each. There are 30 total.

If you added another group of 10, there would be 40 sticks.

Directions: Use the groups of 5 sticks to answer the questions.

1 How many groups of 5 sticks are there? _____

2 How many sticks are there in total? _____

3 How many groups of 5 can you sort 30 sticks into? _____

4 Start with 4 groups of sticks. How many is that? _____

5 Add 1 more group of sticks to the total you found in the last question. How many is the new total? _____

Name: _____ Date: _____

More Sticky Groups!

Many numbers can divided up into equal amounts. For example, this group of sticks has been sorted into 10 groups of 7 sticks each. There are 70 total.

Directions: Use the groups of 7 sticks to answer the questions.

1 How many equal groups of 7 can you sort 70 sticks into? _____

2 How many equal groups of 7 can you sort 35 sticks into? _____

3 Start with 2 groups of sticks. How many is that? _____
Add 1 more group of sticks to the total.
How many is the new total? _____

4 Start with 4 groups of sticks. How many is that? _____
Add 1 more group of sticks to the total.
How many is the new total? _____

5 Start with 5 groups of sticks. How many is that? _____
Add 1 more group of sticks to the total.
How many is the new total? _____

6 Start with 8 groups of sticks. How many is that? _____
Add 1 more group of sticks to the total.
How many is the new total? _____

Name: _____ **Date:** _____

Money Problems

. . . .

Directions: Use the $20.00 bills above to solve the problems.

1 Char has $60.00. She gives her brother $20.00 and her sister $20.00. How much does she have left? _____

2 Kurt has $80.00. He has four friends with birthdays. How much can he spend on each friend? _____

3 Barb has two sons. She has $40.00 for their lunch money. How much does each son get? _____

Directions: Use the $5.00 bills above to solve the problems.

4 Tom takes $5.00 to work each day for his lunch. How much does he need for 5 days? _____

Write the equation that shows this problem:
_____ × _____ = _____

5 Marnie saves $5.00 each week for a new sweater. She has saved for 3 weeks. She needs $25.00. How much has she saved? _____ How much more does she need? _____

Name: _____ **Date:** _____

Got Milk?

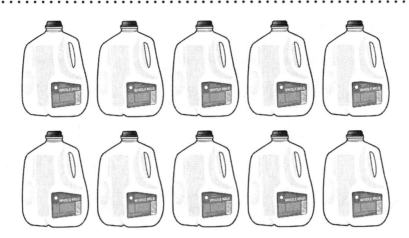

Directions: Use the milk gallons to solve the problems.

1 Each jug holds a gallon of milk. How many gallons are there in total?
_____

Write the equation that shows this problem:

_____ × _____ = _____

2 Dan's family drinks 2 gallons of milk a week. How many gallons will they drink in 4 weeks? _____

Show how to write this as a multiplication problem:

_____ × _____ = _____

3 Each gallon of milk costs $2.00. How much do 5 gallons cost? _____

4 Marta's family drinks 3 gallons of milk a week. How many gallons will they drink in 3 weeks? _____

Show how to write this as a multiplication problem:

_____ × _____ = _____

Name: _____ **Date:** _____

Missing Multipliers

Directions: Find the missing number in each problem.

1 2 × _____ = 10	**2** 8 × _____ = 80	**3** 5 × _____ = 30
4 6 × _____ = 18	**5** 9 × _____ = 72	**6** 8 × _____ = 32
7 5 × _____ = 30	**8** 9 × _____ = 81	**9** 9 × _____ = 54
10 2 × _____ = 14	**11** 11 × _____ = 99	**12** 3 × _____ = 27
13 6 × _____ = 24	**14** 7 × _____ = 56	**15** 9 × _____ = 36
16 4 × _____ = 36	**17** 9 × _____ = 72	**18** 11 × _____ = 55

Name: _____ **Date:** _____

More Missing Multipliers

Directions: Find the missing number in each problem.

1 $9 \times \underline{\hspace{1cm}} = 72$	**2** $8 \times \underline{\hspace{1cm}} = 80$	**3** $7 \times \underline{\hspace{1cm}} = 70$
4 $4 \times \underline{\hspace{1cm}} = 36$	**5** $5 \times \underline{\hspace{1cm}} = 45$	**6** $7 \times \underline{\hspace{1cm}} = 14$
7 $2 \times \underline{\hspace{1cm}} = 10$	**8** $3 \times \underline{\hspace{1cm}} = 33$	**9** $11 \times \underline{\hspace{1cm}} = 99$
10 $9 \times \underline{\hspace{1cm}} = 81$	**11** $7 \times \underline{\hspace{1cm}} = 56$	**12** $7 \times \underline{\hspace{1cm}} = 14$
13 $3 \times \underline{\hspace{1cm}} = 15$	**14** $7 \times \underline{\hspace{1cm}} = 35$	**15** $1 \times \underline{\hspace{1cm}} = 8$
16 $5 \times \underline{\hspace{1cm}} = 35$	**17** $5 \times \underline{\hspace{1cm}} = 50$	**18** $2 \times \underline{\hspace{1cm}} = 2$

Name: _____ **Date:** _____

Missing Numbers

Directions: Find the missing number in each problem.

1 $16 - \underline{\hspace{1cm}} = 14$	**2** $6 \times \underline{\hspace{1cm}} = 18$	**3** $26 - \underline{\hspace{1cm}} = 12$
4 $9 \times \underline{\hspace{1cm}} = 81$	**5** $10 + \underline{\hspace{1cm}} = 44$	**6** $2 \times \underline{\hspace{1cm}} = 24$
7 $10 \times \underline{\hspace{1cm}} = 110$	**8** $4 \times \underline{\hspace{1cm}} = 24$	**9** $6 \times \underline{\hspace{1cm}} = 24$
10 $18 + \underline{\hspace{1cm}} = 20$	**11** $25 + \underline{\hspace{1cm}} = 40$	**12** $4 \times \underline{\hspace{1cm}} = 36$
13 $15 - \underline{\hspace{1cm}} = 8$	**14** $7 \times \underline{\hspace{1cm}} = 42$	**15** $3 \times \underline{\hspace{1cm}} = 12$
16 $10 + \underline{\hspace{1cm}} = 24$	**17** $7 \times \underline{\hspace{1cm}} = 70$	**18** $11 \times \underline{\hspace{1cm}} = 44$

#50886—Bright & Brainy: 3rd Grade Practice

Name: _____ **Date:** _____

Multiply Either Way

The **Commutative Property of Multiplication** states that when the order of the factors is changed, the product stays the same.

Examples:

$3 \times 6 = 6 \times 3$

$3 \times 6 = 18$

$6 \times 3 = 18$

$\begin{array}{r} 6 \\ \underline{\times\ 3} \\ 18 \end{array}$ $\begin{array}{r} 3 \\ \underline{\times\ 6} \\ 18 \end{array}$

Directions: Find the answers to the sets of multiplication problems.

❶ $2 \times 8 = 8 \times$ _____ $2 \times 8 =$ _____ $8 \times 2 =$ _____	**❷** $1 \times 6 = 6 \times$ _____ $1 \times 6 =$ _____ $6 \times 1 =$ _____	**❸** $7 \times 2 =$ _____ $\times 7$ $7 \times 2 =$ _____ $2 \times 7 =$ _____
❹ $3 \times 4 = 4 \times$ _____ $3 \times 4 =$ _____ $4 \times 3 =$ _____	**❺** $4 \times 2 = 2 \times$ _____ $4 \times 2 =$ _____ $2 \times 4 =$ _____	**❻** $10 \times 0 =$ _____ $\times 10$ $10 \times 0 =$ _____ $0 \times 10 =$ _____
❼ $7 \times 8 = 8 \times$ _____ $7 \times 8 =$ _____ $8 \times 7 =$ _____	**❽** $3 \times 5 = 5 \times$ _____ $3 \times 5 =$ _____ $5 \times 3 =$ _____	**❾** $11 \times 2 =$ _____ $\times 11$ $11 \times 2 =$ _____ $2 \times 11 =$ _____
❿ $6 \times 4 = 4 \times$ _____ $4 \times 6 =$ _____ $6 \times 4 =$ _____	**⓫** $1 \times 9 = 9 \times$ _____ $1 \times 9 =$ _____ $9 \times 1 =$ _____	**⓬** $5 \times 6 =$ _____ $\times 5$ $5 \times 6 =$ _____ $6 \times 5 =$ _____

Name: _____ **Date:** _____

Associative Property of Multiplication at Work

The **Associative Property of Multiplication** states that when the grouping of the factors is changed, the product stays the same. The way the factors are grouped does not affect the answers.

Example:

$4 \times (6 \times 2) = (2 \times 6) \times 4$

$4 \times (6 \times 2) = 48$

$(2 \times 6) \times 4 = 48$

Directions: Solve each problem.

❶

$(6 \times 2) \times 3$

_____ × 3 = _____

❷

$(1 \times 22) \times 2$

_____ × 2 = _____

❸

$(1 \times 3) \times 9$

_____ × 9 = _____

❹

$(3 \times 2) \times 4$

_____ × 4 = _____

❺

$(2 \times 2) \times 7$

_____ × 7 = _____

❻

$(7 \times 3) \times 5$

_____ × 5 = _____

❼

$(2 \times 20) \times 6$

_____ × 6 = _____

❽

$(10 \times 3) \times 7$

_____ × 7 = _____

Name: _____ **Date:** _____

Multiply in Steps!

Directions: Use the Associative Property of Multiplication to solve each problem.

①

$$9 \times (2 \times 4)$$

$9 \times$ _____ = _____

②

$$4 \times (1 \times 9)$$

$4 \times$ _____ = _____

③

$$3 \times (40 \times 2)$$

$3 \times$ _____ = _____

④

$$7 \times (1 \times 6)$$

$7 \times$ _____ = _____

⑤

$$5 \times (1 \times 11)$$

$5 \times$ _____ = _____

⑥

$$2 \times (12 \times 5)$$

$2 \times$ _____ = _____

⑦

$$8 \times (10 \times 2)$$

$8 \times$ _____ = _____

⑧

$$9 \times (2 \times 5)$$

$9 \times$ _____ = _____

Name: _____ **Date:** _____

Choose the Steps!

Directions: Use the Associative Property of Multiplication to solve each problem.

❶

$3 \times 2 \times 4$

_____ × _____ = _____

❷

$2 \times 12 \times 1$

_____ × _____ = _____

❸

$4 \times 3 \times 5$

_____ × _____ = _____

❹

$2 \times 5 \times 3$

_____ × _____ = _____

❺

$10 \times 8 \times 2$

_____ × _____ = _____

❻

$6 \times 8 \times 1$

_____ × _____ = _____

❼

$5 \times 4 \times 1$

_____ × _____ = _____

❽

$4 \times 3 \times 9$

_____ × _____ = _____

Name: _____ **Date:** _____

Divide Up the Sticks!

100 sticks have been divided into 10 equal groups.

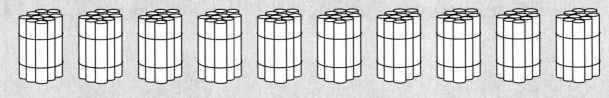

$$10 \times 10 = 100$$

Use the factors in the multiplication problem to figure out the division problem:

$$100 \div 10 = 10$$

Directions: Solve each problem. Use the sticks above to help you.

❶

$$10 \times \underline{\hspace{1cm}} = 80$$

$$80 \div 10 = \underline{\hspace{1cm}}$$

❷

$$10 \times \underline{\hspace{1cm}} = 50$$

$$50 \div 10 = \underline{\hspace{1cm}}$$

❸

$$10 \times \underline{\hspace{1cm}} = 20$$

$$20 \div 10 = \underline{\hspace{1cm}}$$

❹

$$10 \times \underline{\hspace{1cm}} = 90$$

$$90 \div 10 = \underline{\hspace{1cm}}$$

Name: _____ **Date:** _____

Multiply and Divide Them Up!

You know from multiplication that 6 x 8 = 48.

You can use the factors in multiplication to figure out division problems:

48 ÷ 6 = _____

You know that the answer is 8 because 6 x 8 = 48.

48 ÷ 6 = __8__

Directions: Solve the problems.

1 3 × _____ = 27 27 ÷ 3 = _____	**2** 2 × _____ = 50 50 ÷ 2 = _____	**3** 5 × _____ = 35 35 ÷ 5 = _____
4 1 × _____ = 12 12 ÷ 1 = _____	**5** 10 × _____ = 40 40 ÷ 10 = _____	**6** 3 × _____ = 30 30 ÷ 3 = _____
7 7 × _____ = 77 77 ÷ 7 = _____	**8** 8 × _____ = 88 88 ÷ 8 = _____	**9** 11 × _____ = 66 66 ÷ 11 = _____

Name: _____ **Date:** _____

More Problems to Multiply and Divide

You know from multiplication that $4 \times 8 = 32$.

You can use the factors in multiplication to figure out division problems:

$$32 \div 4 = \underline{\hspace{1cm}}$$

You know that the answer is 8 because $4 \times 8 = 32$.

$$32 \div 4 = \underline{\ 8\ }$$

Directions: Solve the problems.

1 $3 \times \underline{\hspace{1.5cm}} = 33$ $33 \div 3 = \underline{\hspace{1.5cm}}$	**2** $6 \times \underline{\hspace{1.5cm}} = 54$ $54 \div 6 = \underline{\hspace{1.5cm}}$	**3** $6 \times \underline{\hspace{1.5cm}} = 36$ $36 \div 6 = \underline{\hspace{1.5cm}}$
4 $2 \times \underline{\hspace{1.5cm}} = 12$ $12 \div 2 = \underline{\hspace{1.5cm}}$	**5** $20 \times \underline{\hspace{1.5cm}} = 80$ $80 \div 20 = \underline{\hspace{1.5cm}}$	**6** $2 \times \underline{\hspace{1.5cm}} = 20$ $20 \div 2 = \underline{\hspace{1.5cm}}$
7 $8 \times \underline{\hspace{1.2cm}} = 88$ $88 \div 8 = \underline{\hspace{1.5cm}}$	**8** $7 \times \underline{\hspace{1.5cm}} = 84$ $84 \div 7 = \underline{\hspace{1.5cm}}$	**9** $8 \times \underline{\hspace{1.5cm}} = 64$ $64 \div 8 = \underline{\hspace{1.5cm}}$

Name: _____ **Date:** _____

Big Problems

To solve word problems with more than one step, it is helpful to show them as a math problem.

Example: Anthony bought jeans for $23.00. He bought a shirt for $17.00.   He had $50.00. How much did he have left?

Here's how to work the problem: $23.00 + $17.00 = $40.00

$40.00 is the total cost of his purchases. He has $50.00.

$50.00 – $40.00 = $10.00 Anthony has $10.00 left.

Directions: Solve each word problem.

---

❶

Edward buys 9 gallons of gas twice a week. On Monday gas is $4.00 per gallon. On Thursday gas is on sale for $3.00 per gallon. How much does the gas cost him for the week?

Step 1: _____ × _____ = _____

Step 2: _____ × _____ = _____

Step 3: _____ + _____ = _____

It cost him $ _____ for the week.

❷

Nathaniel climbed North Maroon Peak, which is 14,014 feet high. Nathaniel also climbed Gray's Peak, which is 14,270 feet high. He wants to climb at least 40,000 feet total this month. How high should the next mountain peak be?

Step 1:

Step 2:

The next mountain peak should be _____ feet.

Name: _____ **Date:** _____

More Big Problems!

To solve word problems with more than one step, it is helpful to show them as a math problem.

Example: Veronica's mom gave her a box of 50 colored pencils. They were divided into 10 different colors. Veronica used up all the pink pencils first. How many did she have left?

Here's how to work the problem:
50 ÷ 10 = 5. There are 5 colors in each group.

50 − 5 = 45. Veronica has 45 pencils left.

Directions: Solve each word problem.

❶

The game board has 86 spaces to land on. Oliver rolls the dice and gets a 6 five times in a row. He rolls two more times and gets a 3 each time. How many more spaces does he need to go to finish the game?

Step 1:

Step 2:

Step 3:

He needs to go _____ more spaces.

❷

A family of 4 wants to go to a baseball game. The tickets cost $11.00 per person. Snacks will cost $6.00 per person. The family has saved $60.00. How many more dollars do they need for the game?

Step 1:

Step 2:

Step 3:

They need $ _____ more.

Name: _____ **Date:** _____

Fraction Fun!

This circle is divided into 2 equal parts. One of these two parts, or one half, is shaded. Another way to say this is $\frac{1}{2}$. The top number in the fraction represents the shaded part. The bottom number represents the 2 parts of the circle.

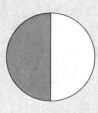

Directions: Write the fraction that tells how many parts are shaded.

❶

_____

❷

_____

❸

_____

❹

_____

❺

_____

❻

_____

Name: _____ **Date:** _____

More Fraction Fun!

This circle shown below is divided into 4 equal parts. Three of the 4 parts, or $\frac{3}{4}$, are shaded. The top number in the fraction represents how many parts are shaded. The bottom number represents the 4 parts the circle is divided into.

Directions: Shade the figure to show the fraction.

❶ $\frac{1}{3}$

❷ $\frac{2}{6}$

❸ $\frac{1}{2}$

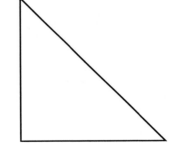

❹ $\frac{1}{2}$

❺ $\frac{2}{4}$

❻ $\frac{3}{4}$

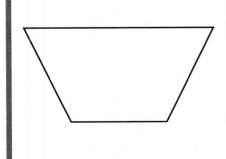
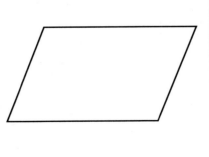
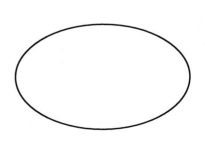

Name: _____ **Date:** _____

Fractions on a Line

A **number line** can be divided into fractional parts. This number line begins at 0 and ends at 1. It shows one unit with four equal parts.

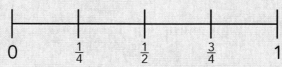

This number line is divided into sections of $\frac{1}{8}$.

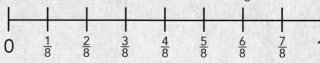

Directions: Look at the number line. Then, answer the questions.

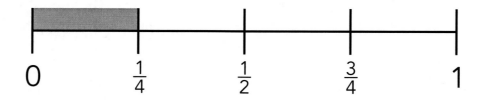

1 How many parts is this number line divided into? _____

2 How many parts are shaded? _____

3 What is the fraction for the shaded parts? _____

Name: _____ **Date:** _____

Line Up for Fractions!

Directions: Mark the number lines as indicated.

1 Write the fractions under the line.

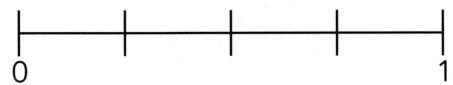

0   1

2 Mark the number line into fifths. Write the fractions under the line.

0 $\frac{5}{5}$

3 Mark the number line into thirds. Write the fractions under the line.

0 $\frac{3}{3}$

4 Mark the number line into sixths. Write the fractions under the lines.

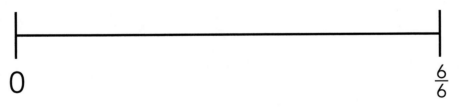

0 $\frac{6}{6}$

Name: _____ **Date:** _____

Find Equal Fractions

Directions: Use the number lines to answer the questions.

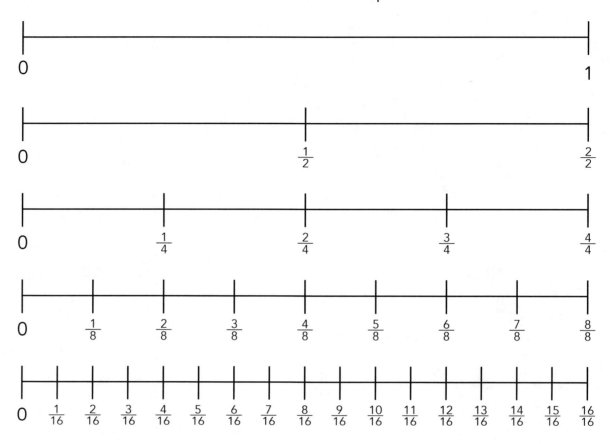

1 How many parts does the first line have? _____

2 How many parts does the second line have? _____

3 How many parts does the third line have? _____

4 How many parts does the fourth line have? _____

5 How many parts does the last line have? _____

6 The fraction $\frac{1}{2}$ lines up with $\frac{2}{4}$. They are equivalent. Name 2 more fractions that equal $\frac{1}{2}$ and $\frac{2}{4}$.

_____ and _____

#50886—Bright & Brainy: 3rd Grade Practice

Name: _____ **Date:** _____

Find Equal and Unequal Fractions

Directions: Use the number lines to answer the questions.

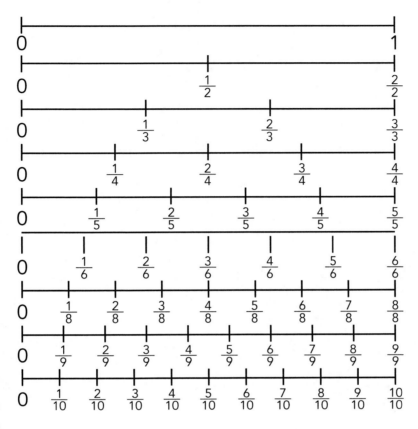

1 The fraction $\frac{1}{2}$ lines up with $\frac{2}{4}$. They are equivalent.

Name 3 more fractions that are equivalent to $\frac{1}{2}$ and $\frac{2}{4}$.

_____, _____, and _____

2 Name 2 more fractions that are equivalent to $\frac{1}{3}$.
_____ and _____

3 Name 1 more fraction that is equivalent to $\frac{2}{5}$. _____

4 Find 2 fractions that have no equivalent fractions.
_____ and _____

Name: _____ **Date:** _____

Make a Fraction Chart

Directions: Write the fractions to show the parts of each unit.

1								

$\frac{1}{2}$ $\frac{1}{2}$

Name: _____ **Date:** _____

Find the Fractions

Directions: Use the fraction chart that you completed on page 182 to answer the questions.

1 Name a fraction or fractions that is equivalent to $\frac{5}{10}$.

_____

2 Name a fraction or fractions that is equivalent to $\frac{6}{10}$.

_____

3 Name a fraction or fractions that is equivalent to $\frac{3}{9}$.

_____

4 Name a fraction or fractions that is equivalent to $\frac{2}{8}$.

_____

5 Name a fraction or fractions that is equivalent to $\frac{7}{7}$.

_____

6 Name a fraction or fractions that is equivalent to $\frac{2}{6}$.

_____

7 Name a fraction or fractions that is equivalent to $\frac{2}{5}$.

_____

8 Name a fraction or fractions that is equivalent to $\frac{1}{4}$.

_____

9 Name a fraction or fractions that is equivalent to $\frac{2}{3}$.

_____

10 Name a fraction or fractions that is equivalent to $\frac{1}{2}$.

_____

Name: _____ **Date:** _____

The Whole Thing

A number that shows an entire item is called a **whole number.**

| There is 1 apple in this box. The fraction for 1 is $\frac{1}{1}$. The whole number is 1. | There are two apples in this box. Two whole apples is $\frac{1}{1}$ + $\frac{1}{1}$ or $\frac{2}{1}$. $\frac{2}{1}$ = 2. The number 2 is the whole number. |

Directions: Answer the questions below.

❶

Write an addition problem to show the apples in fractions:
_____

What is the whole number? _____

❷

Write an addition problem to show the apples in fractions:
_____

What is the whole number? _____

❸

Write an addition problem to show the apples in fractions:
_____

What is the whole number? _____

Name: _____ **Date:** _____

Mix It Up!

When a number has a whole number, such as 1, plus a fraction, it is called a **mixed number**.

Example:

| There is 1 apple in this box. The fraction for 1 is $\frac{1}{1}$. The whole number is 1. | There are two halves in this box. The fraction for 2 halves is $\frac{2}{2}$. | There is one whole apple and $\frac{1}{2}$ apple in this box. The fraction for 1 whole apple and $\frac{1}{2}$ apple is $1\frac{1}{2}$. |

Directions: Circle whether a whole number or a mixed number is shown. Then, write the number on the line.

1    whole   mixed   _____

2    whole   mixed   _____

3    whole   mixed   _____

4    whole   mixed   _____

5    whole   mixed   _____

Name: _____ **Date:** _____

What's the Size?

Directions: Compare the fractions. Write <, > or = inside the circle.

1

$\dfrac{1}{8}$ ◯ $\dfrac{1}{4}$

2

$\dfrac{1}{3}$ ◯ $\dfrac{1}{6}$

3

$\dfrac{5}{6}$ ◯ $\dfrac{1}{3}$

4

$\dfrac{4}{8}$ ◯ $\dfrac{1}{2}$

Name: _____ **Date:** _____

Compare Sizes

Directions: Compare the fractions. Write <, > or = inside the circle.

1 Write the fraction that is shaded.

_____ ◯ _____

2 Write the fraction that is shaded.

_____ ◯ _____

3 Write the fraction that is shaded.

_____ ◯ _____

4 Write the fraction that is shaded.

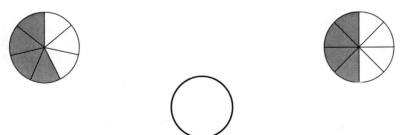

_____ ◯ _____

Name: _____ **Date:** _____

Compare Sizes of Fractions

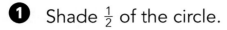

Directions: Compare the fractions. Write <, > or = inside the circle.

1 Shade $\frac{1}{2}$ of the circle.   Shade $\frac{3}{8}$ of the circle.

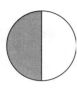

2 Shade $\frac{3}{6}$ of the circle.   Shade $\frac{1}{2}$ of the circle.

     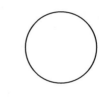

3 Shade $\frac{3}{4}$ of the circle.   Shade $\frac{5}{8}$ of the circle.

4 Shade $\frac{1}{3}$ of the circle.   Shade $\frac{1}{2}$ of the circle.

© Shell Education

Name: _____ **Date:** _____

Tell Time

Directions: Draw the hands on the clocks to show the starting and ending times. Write the times on the lines. Then, answer the questions.

	Starting Time	Ending Time
1 Charmaine started jogging at 7:10 A.M. She jogged for 20 minutes. What time did she finish jogging? _____	____ : ____ ____	____ : ____ ____
2 Dawson went to work at 9:00 A.M. He worked for 4 hours and 30 minutes. What time did he finish work? _____	____ : ____ ____	____ : ____ ____
3 Freddy started picking up trash at 11:45 A.M. He finished 2 hours and 15 minutes later. What time did he finish picking up trash? _____	____ : ____ ____	____ : ____ ____
4 Gary's party ended at 10:00 P.M. It lasted $3\frac{1}{2}$ hours. What time did the party start? _____	____ : ____ ____	____ : ____ ____

Name: _____ **Date:** _____

How Much Time?

Directions: Draw the hands on the clocks to show the starting and ending times. Write the times on the lines. Then, answer the questions.

1 Kendra started swimming at 6:20 A.M. She ended at 7:10 A.M. How many minutes did she swim? _____	**Starting Time** 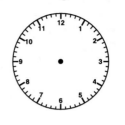 ____ : ___ ___	**Ending Time** 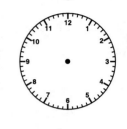 ____ : ___ ___
2 Louanne started school at 8:30 A.M. She ended at 3:45 P.M. How many hours and minutes was she at school? _____ hours _____ minutes	**Starting Time** 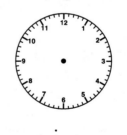 ____ : ___ ___	**Ending Time** 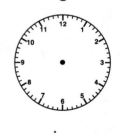 ____ : ___ ___
3 Owen started delivering flyers at 8:15 A.M. on Saturday. At 11:45 A.M., he needed to stop working so he could leave for a game. How many hours and minutes could he work? _____ hours _____ minutes	**Starting Time** 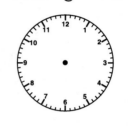 ____ : ___ ___	**Ending Time** 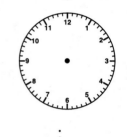 ____ : ___ ___
4 Rana has to go to bed at 9:00 P.M. She started her homework at 7:45 P.M. How many hours and minutes could she work? _____ hours _____ minutes	**Starting Time**  ____ : ___ ___	**Ending Time** 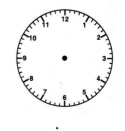 ____ : ___ ___

Name: _____ Date: _____

Measure Liters

Directions: Circle the best answer to the question.

> A **liter** is a metric unit of volume. A shampoo bottle is usually a liter, a soda bottle is usually 2 liters, and a bucket can hold about 5 liters.

1 About how many liters would you need to fill a pet cat's bowl?

   a. 1

   b. 5

   c. 10

2 About how many liters of water would you need to wash your hands?

   a. 2

   b. 5

   c. 10

3 About how many liters of gas are needed to fill a car's gas tank?

   a. 5

   b. 10

   c. 40

4 About how many liters of milk are needed for a baby's cup?

   a. $\frac{1}{2}$

   b. 2

   c. 5

5 About how many liters of juice are needed to fill a large punch bowl?

   a. 1

   b. 5

   c. 10

Name: _____ **Date:** _____

Weighing Grams and Kilograms

A **gram** (g) is very light. A dollar bill weighs about 1 gram.

A **kilogram** (kg) equals 1,000 grams. A kilogram is a little more than 2 pounds. That's about the same as a liter of water.

Directions: Would you use grams (g) or kilograms (kg) to weigh the object? Circle *g* for grams and *kg* for kilograms.

1 sock g kg	**2** paperclip g kg
3 full bag of trash g kg	**4** stamp g kg
5 television g kg	**6** bike g kg
7 envelope g kg	**8** earrings g kg
9 backpack full of books g kg	**10** penny g kg

Name: _____ **Date:** _____

Graph those Worms!

Directions: Draw *X*s to show how many worms each person collected.

Worms collected
Dad—10
Mom—7
Jeanine—5
Pedro—8
Matthew—6
Zenia—12
Patsy—9

Names	Number of worms collected
Zenia	
Dad	
Patsy	
Pedro	
Mom	
Matthew	
Jeanine	

1 How many worms did Mom and Dad collect? _____

2 How many worms did the rest collect? _____

3 Which two people collected the most worms? _____

4 How many did those two people collect in total? _____

5 How many worms did everyone collect in total? _____

Name: _____ **Date:** _____

Bar Graph

Directions: Use the bar graph to answer the questions.

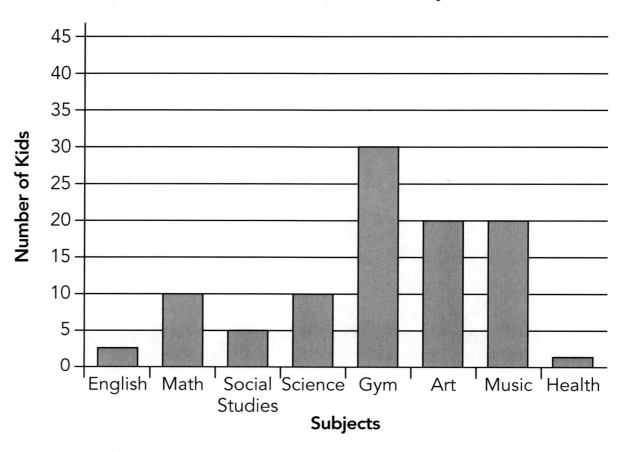

Kids' Favorite School Subject

1 How many kids like gym for their favorite subject? _____

2 How many kids like art for their favorite subject? _____

3 What subject is liked least? _____

4 What subject is liked best by exactly 10 kids? _____

5 How many students took the survey? _____

Name: _____ **Date:** _____

Create Your Own Bar Graph

Directions: Use the blank chart to do a survey of your friends about their favorites. Use the model on the previous page to help you.

Here are the steps:

1 First choose the topic.

2 Write the categories across the bottom.

3 Ask up to 15 people which is their favorite of the choices.

4 Total up the responses for each choice.

5 Create your chart by drawing bars.

Name: _____ **Date:** _____

Measure Up!

Directions: Find each item on the list. Measure it with the ruler. Then, record the number of inches.

Item to measure	Number of inches
1 length of paper clip	_____ in.
2 length of cell phone	_____ in.
3 length of book	_____ in.
4 length of notebook	_____ in.
5 width of CD case	_____ in.
6 length of magazine	_____ in.
7 length of your nose	_____ in.
8 length of pencil	_____ in.
9 height of water bottle	_____ in.
10 length of your thumb	_____ in.

Name: _____ **Date:** _____

Measure by the Foot!

Directions: Find each item on the list. Measure it with the yardstick.
Round each answer to the nearest half foot.

Item to measure	Number of feet
1 height of wastebasket	_____ ft.
2 width of chair seat	_____ ft.
3 length of your bed	_____ ft.
4 length of a rug	_____ ft.
5 length of a square in a sidewalk	_____ ft.
6 length of a shelf	_____ ft.
7 height of a television	_____ ft.
8 length of kitchen counter	_____ ft.
9 length of computer	_____ ft.
10 length of a towel	_____ ft.

Name: _____ **Date:** _____

What About Area?

There are 4 squares in this shape. The area is 4 square units.

```
1 2
3 4
```

Directions: Find the area of each shape.

1

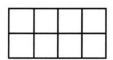

_____ square units

2

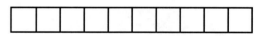

_____ square units

3

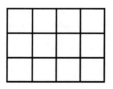

_____ square units

4

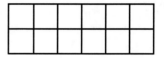

_____ square units

5

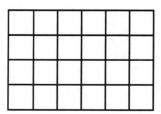

_____ square units

6

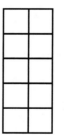

_____ square units

7

_____ square units

8

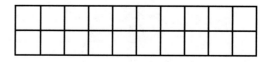

_____ square units

Name: _____ **Date:** _____

Find the Area

The area is the number of square units (inches, centimeters, feet) in a shape. Count the number of units in the shape to find the area.

There are 3 square centimeters in this shape. The area is 3 square centimeters.

```
1 2
3
```

Directions: Find the area of each shape. Each box represents 1 square centimeter.

1

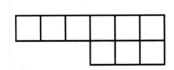

_____ square cm

2

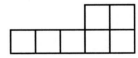

_____ square cm

3

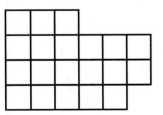

_____ square cm

4

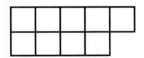

_____ square cm

5

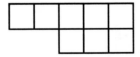

_____ square cm

6

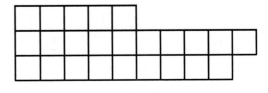

_____ square cm

Name: _____ **Date:** _____

The Area Formula

 The area of this shape is 6 square units. The width on one side is 2 tiles and the length of the other side is 3 tiles. The area of a rectangle is equal to length times width.

The formula is $A = l \times w$.

You can compute the area of this rectangle in this way:

2 × 3 = _____ (area)

2 × 3 = _____ square units

Directions: Find the area of each shape.

❶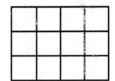

The width is _____ square units.
The length is _____ square units.

_____ × _____ = _____ square units

❷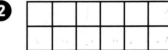

The width is _____ square units.
The length is _____ square units.

_____ × _____ = _____ square units

❸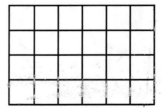

The width is _____ square units.
The length is _____ square units.

_____ × _____ = _____ square units

❹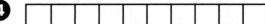

The width is _____ square units.
The length is _____ square units.

_____ × _____ = _____ square units

Name: _____ Date: _____

Measure the Area

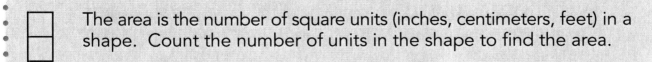

The area is the number of square units (inches, centimeters, feet) in a shape. Count the number of units in the shape to find the area.

Each side of this square stands for 1 foot. The width is 1 foot. The length is 2 feet. The square represents 2 square feet.

You can compute the area of a rectangle in this way:

$1 \times 2 =$ _____ (area)

$1 \times 2 =$ _____ square feet

Directions: Find the area of each shape with a ruler or yardstick. Round the inches to the nearest foot.

---

❶ Measure the area of the top of a desk.

Width = _____ square feet
Length = _____ square feet

_____ × _____ = _____ square feet

---

❷ Measure the area of a kitchen counter.

Width = _____ square feet
Length = _____ square feet

_____ × _____ = _____ square feet

---

❸ Measure the area of the top of your bed.

Width = _____ square feet
Length = _____ square feet

_____ × _____ = _____ square feet

---

❹ Measure the area of a door.

Width = _____ square feet
Length = _____ square feet

_____ × _____ = _____ square feet

Name: _____ **Date:** _____

Measure More Areas

The area is the number of square units (inches, centimeters, feet) in a shape. Count the number of units in the shape to find the area. The formula is $A = l \times w$

Directions: Find the area of each shape with a ruler or yardstick. Round to the nearest foot or inch depending on which unit of measure you use.

❶ Measure the area of a cereal box.

Width = _____ square _____
Length = _____ square _____

_____ × _____ = _____ square _____

❷ Measure the area of a bathroom counter.

Width = _____ square _____
Length = _____ square _____

_____ × _____ = _____ square _____

❸ Measure the area of a sink.

Width = _____ square _____
Length = _____ square _____

_____ × _____ = _____ square _____

❹ Measure the area of a floor rug.

Width = _____ square _____
Length = _____ square _____

_____ × _____ = _____ square _____

Name: _____ **Date:** _____

Problem Areas!

Directions: Solve the problems below using the formula for finding area. Remember, the formula is $A = l \times w$.

1 Brett and Angie share a driveway. They need to replace it. They want to share the costs equally. The driveway is 20 feet by 12 feet. For how many square feet will each have to pay?

_____ × _____ = _____ square feet

_____ ÷ 2 = _____ square feet

2 Martin and Benjamin are twins and share a bedroom. They want to divide it equally. The bedroom is 9 feet by 12 feet. How many square feet will each twin get?

_____ × _____ = _____ square feet

_____ ÷ _____ = _____ square feet

Their beds are each about 4 feet by 8 feet. How many square feet is each bed?

_____ × _____ = _____ square feet

How many square feet of floor space remains after the beds are placed?

Each twin has _____ square feet left.

Name: _____ **Date:** _____

More Problem Areas!

....

Directions: Solve the problems below using the formula for finding area. Remember, the formula is $A = l \times w$.

---

1 Alesha and Amy are twins. They are moving into a new house. Each wants to have the biggest bedroom. Bedroom 1 is 10 feet by 13 feet. Bedroom 2 is 11 feet by 12 feet. What is the size of each bedroom?

Bedroom 1: _____ × _____ = _____ square feet

Bedroom 2: _____ × _____ = _____ square feet

Which bedroom is bigger? _____

How many square feet bigger is it? _____ square feet

---

2 Annie is replacing her kitchen and bathroom counters. The kitchen counters are 2 feet by 5 feet and 2 feet by 6 feet. She needs 2 bathroom counters. Each bathroom counter is 2 feet by 3 feet. How many square feet of counter top will she need?

Kitchen: _____ × _____ = _____ square feet

Kitchen: _____ × _____ = _____ square feet

Bathroom _____ × _____ = _____ square feet

Bathroom _____ × _____ = _____ square feet

She needs _____ square feet of granite.

Most slabs of granite are 10 feet by 6 feet.

Granite: _____ × _____ = _____ square feet

Will there be enough granite in one slab? _____

Name: _____ **Date:** _____

Still More Problem Areas!

Directions: Solve the problems below using the formula for finding area. Remember, the formula is $A = l \times w$.

---

❶ Angelo is replacing one side of his fence. The length is 96 feet. Each panel is 6 feet wide.

How many panels will he need?

_____ ÷ _____ = _____ panels

Each panel is 6 feet wide and 8 feet high. How many square feet is in each panel?

_____ × _____ = _____ square feet

How many square feet of boards will he have for his fence?

_____ × _____ = _____ square feet

---

❷ Patricia is selling her apartment. She needs to find out its total square footage.

The bedroom is 12 feet by 15 feet. The kitchen is 11 feet by 13 feet. The living room is 14 feet by 15 feet. The bathroom is 8 feet by 7 feet.

Bedroom: _____ × _____ = _____ square feet

Kitchen: _____ × _____ = _____ square feet

Living room: _____ × _____ = _____ square feet

Bathroom: _____ × _____ = _____ square feet

What is the total square footage? _____

Name: _____ **Date:** _____

Computing Irregular Areas

It takes 3 steps to compute the area of this figure.

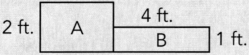

3 ft.

2 ft. | A

4 ft.

B | 1 ft.

Think of the shape as having two sections. Section A is 3 feet by 2 feet.
3 × 2 = 6.

Section B is 4 feet by 1 foot. 4 × 1 = 4.

Add the 2 sections to compute the total area.
6 + 4 = 10 square feet.

Directions: Compute the areas of these shapes. Show all three steps.

❶

1 ft.

A

5 ft.

B | 4 ft.

2 ft.

Section A: _____ feet × _____ feet = _____ square foot

Section B: _____ feet × _____ feet = _____ square feet

_____ + _____ = _____ square feet

❷

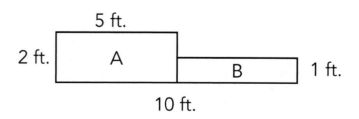

5 ft.

2 ft. | A

B | 1 ft.

10 ft.

Section A: _____ feet × _____ feet = _____ square feet

Section B: _____ feet × _____ feet = _____ square feet

_____ + _____ = _____ square feet

Name: _____ **Date:** _____

More Irregular Area Computations

It takes 3 steps to compute the area of this figure.

3 ft.

2 ft. | A | 4 ft.
B | 1 ft.

Think of the shape as having two sections. Section A is 3 feet by 2 feet.
$3 \times 2 = 6$.

Section B is 4 feet by 1 foot. $4 \times 1 = 4$.

Add the 2 sections to compute the total area.
$6 + 4 = 10$ square feet.

1

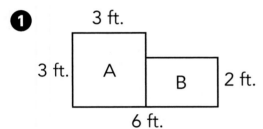

Section A: _____ feet × _____ feet = _____ square feet

Section B: _____ feet × _____ feet = _____ square feet

_____ + _____ = _____ square feet

2

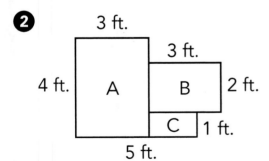

Section A: _____ feet × _____ feet = _____ square feet

Section B: _____ feet × _____ feet = _____ square feet

Section C: _____ feet × _____ feet = _____ square feet

_____ + _____ + _____ = _____ square feet

Name: _____ **Date:** _____

Perimeter

The **perimeter** is the outside measurement of a shape. To find the perimeter, count the number of inches on each side of the shape. Then, add all the sides together.

Directions: Find the perimeter for each shape.

1

4 in.

3 in.

Perimeter = _____ inches

2

10 in.

2 in.

Perimeter = _____ inches

3

10 in.

1 in.

Perimeter = _____ inches

4

6 in.

3 in.

Perimeter = _____ inches

#50886—Bright & Brainy: 3rd Grade Practice

Name: _____ **Date:** _____

More Perimeters

> The **perimeter** is the outside measurement of a shape. To find the perimeter, count the number of inches on each side of the shape. Then, add all the sides together.

Directions: Find the perimeter for each shape.

❶

5 in.

2 in.

1 in.

10 in.

Perimeter = _____ inches

❷

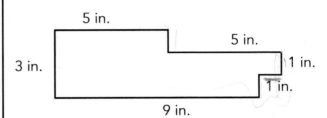

Perimeter = _____ inches

❸

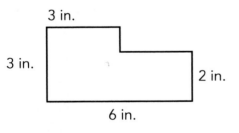

Perimeter = _____ inches

❹

3 in.

4 in.

3 in.

6 in.

Perimeter = _____ inches

Name: _____ **Date:** _____

Some More Perimeters

The **perimeter** is the outside measurement of a shape. To find the perimeter, count the number of inches on each side of the shape. Then, add all the sides together.

Directions: Find the perimeter for each shape.

❶

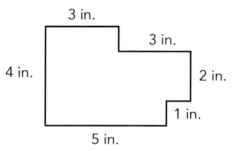

Perimeter = _____ inches

❷

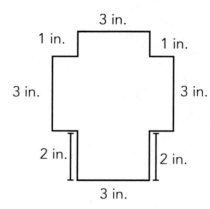

Perimeter = _____ inches

❸

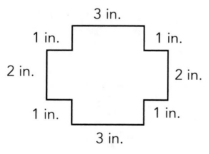

Perimeter = _____ inches

❹

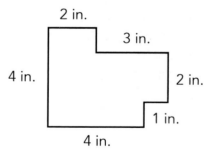

Perimeter = _____ inches

Name: _____ Date: _____

Identify Polygons

Facts about polygons:

- A polygon is a flat enclosed shape.

- A polygon has 3 or more straight sides.

- Polygons are named by the number of sides and angles they have.

- A regular polygon is one in which all sides are equal and all angles are equal.

Directions: Find the regular polygons. Outline each with a crayon or marker.

Name: _____ **Date:** _____

Identify Quadrilaterals

Facts about quadrilaterals:

- A quadrilateral is a polygon with 4 sides.

- The interior angles may or may not be equal.

- The interior angles always add up to 360 degrees.

Directions: Find the quadrilaterals. Outline each with a crayon or marker.

#50886—Bright & Brainy: 3rd Grade Practice   © *Shell Education*

Name: _____ **Date:** _____

Find Shapes

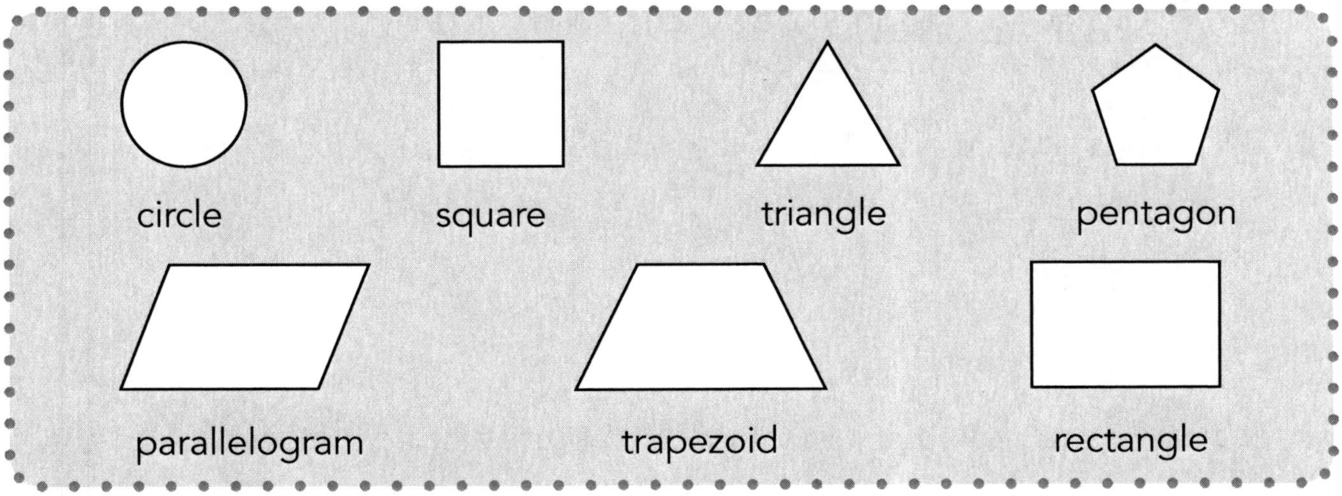

circle　　square　　triangle　　pentagon

parallelogram　　trapezoid　　rectangle

Directions: Find things in your house, school, or neighborhood that have these shapes. Write the name of the shape and the object in the chart.

Shape Name	Object Name

Name: _____ **Date:** _____

Divide These Shapes

Directions: Circles and rectangles can be divided into equal parts. Look at the shapes. Then, answer the questions.

1 Divide this circle in half. It should have 2 equal parts. Color $\frac{1}{2}$ of the circle.

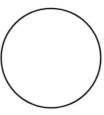

2 Divide this parallelogram into 2 equal parts. Color $\frac{1}{2}$ of the parallelogram.

3 Divide this rectangle into 3 equal parts. Color $\frac{2}{3}$ of the rectangle.

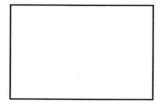

4 Divide this hexagon into 6 equal parts. Color $\frac{1}{3}$ of the hexagon.

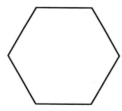

5 Divide this trapezoid into 2 equal parts. Color $\frac{1}{2}$ of the trapezoid.

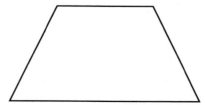

References Cited

Annis, L. F., and D. B. Annis. 1987. *Does practice make perfect? The effects of repetition on student learning.* Paper presented at the annual meeting of the American Educational Research Association, Washington, DC.

Marzano, R. 2010. When practice makes perfect...sense. *Educational Leadership* (68):81–83.

National Governors Association Center for Best Practices and Council of Chief State School Officers. 2010. Common core standards. http://www.corestandards.org/the-standards.

Answer Key

Prefix Challenge (page 11)

1. mistreat
2. impolite
3. impure
4. misbehaved
5. impatient

Suffix Challenges (page 12)

1. itchy
2. builder
3. painter
4. frosty
5. tricky

More Suffix Challenges (page 13)

1. operation
2. direction
3. usable
4. believable
5. addition

Prefix and Suffix Round Up (page 14)

1. wrong
2. make something clean again
3. something that can be laundered
4. something that can be twisted
5. something that can be enjoyed
6. straighten
7. hate
8. make firm
9. honest
10. make limp

Decode Multisyllabic Words (page 15)

1. at/tic
2. can/not
3. com/mon
4. cot/tage
5. cot/ton
6. dol/lar
7. fat/ten
8. fos/sil
9. gal/lon
10. gos/sip

Decode More Multisyllabic Words (page 16)

1. cac/tus
2. con/tent
3. den/tist
4. for/got
5. hel/met
6. hun/dred
7. hus/band
8. mas/ter
9. men/tal
10. mis/take

Spelling Challenges (page 17)

1. several
2. already
3. quiet
4. could
5. balloon
6. aunt
7. instead
8. fourth
9. choose
10. enough

Answer Key (cont.)

More Spelling Challenges (page 18)

1. among
2. cupboard
3. early
4. together
5. sugar
6. children
7. weather
8. quite
9. along
10. country

Name That Noun! (page 19)

1. Mary Jane; horse; race
2. we; chores; race
3. Mary Jane; horse
4. Dad; gas; car
5. Josh; firewood; fire
6. Max; clothes
7. I; clothes; drawers
8. Mom; matches; fire
9. we; hot dogs; marshmallows
10. we; moon; stars

Noun Search (page 20)

1. family; island; vacation
2. we; ferry; lake
3. Dad; car; ferry
4. we; cabin; boat; night
5. ferry; dock
6. Annie; I; tents; beach
7. Mom; I; lunch
8. we; swimsuits; rafts
9. Annie; I; waves
10. Mom; Dad; rafts

Acting Up! (page 21)

1. Students' sentences will vary. Suggested answer: The girl slides down the slide. (circle slides)
2. Students' sentences will vary. Suggested answer: The boy swings the bat. (circle swings)
3. Students' sentences will vary. Suggested answer: The cat licks its whiskers. (circle licks)
4. Students' sentences will vary. Suggested answer: The bird flies in the sky. (circle flies)
5. Students' sentences will vary. Suggested answer: The boy eats a banana. (circle eats)

All About Action (page 22)

1. dine
2. munches
3. laps
4. slurp
5. chew
6. gobbles
7. chomps
8. nibbles
9. bit
10. snack

Noun or Verb? (page 23)

Nouns: ant, April, sky, camera, eagle, holiday, joy, meal, ribbon, spider

Verbs: add, arrive, behave, decide, exclaim, forgive, imagine, notice, prepare, prove

Answer Key (cont.)

Amazing Adjectives (page 24)
1. Students' answers will vary.
2. Students' answers will vary.
3. Students' answers will vary.
4. circle *scary*
5. circle *huge*
6. circle *brave*
7. circle *slimy*
8. circle *pale*

Adjective Fun (page 25)
Students' answers will vary, but all of the answers should be adjectives.

Adverb Action (page 26)
1. Students' answers will vary.
2. Students' answers will vary.
3. Students' answers will vary.
4. Students' answers will vary.
5. Students' answers will vary.
6. Students' answers will vary.
7. Students' answers will vary.
8. Students' answers will vary.
9. Students' answers will vary.
10. Students' answers will vary.

Adverbs (page 27)
1. yesterday
2. outside
3. always
4. never
5. first; north
6. again
7. next
8. forever
9. next
10. yearly

Adjective or Adverb? (page 28)
Adjectives: awful, different, fancy, gentle, greedy, pleasant, quick, sleepy, ugly

Adverbs: already, below, easily, exactly, greedily, outdoors, safely, there, today

Making Words Plural (page 29)
1. boys
2. nickels
3. treasures
4. shirts
5. giants
6. spiders
7. wives
8. dwarves
9. hooves
10. leaves
11. scarves
12. elves

Making More Words Plural (page 30)
1. babies
2. fairies
3. studies
4. cities
5. butterflies
6. bunnies
7. daddies
8. companies
9. candies
10. patties
11. twenties
12. strawberries

Answer Key (cont.)

Making Words Plural with -es (page 31)

1. kisses
2. patches
3. churches
4. beaches
5. coaches
6. sixes
7. washes
8. crashes
9. riches
10. axes
11. passes
12. scratches

Oh No! O-Word Plurals (page 32)

1. heroes
2. volcanoes
3. potatoes
4. tomatoes
5. echoes
6. zeroes
7. cellos
8. tornados
9. mangos
10. memos
11. photos
12. pianos

Sort the Nouns (page 33)

Concrete nouns: ant, bowl, calendar, flame, jar, knight, passenger, policeman, rooster, spoon

Abstract nouns: bravery, comfort, curiosity, difference, fear, laughter, power, pride, shy, truth

More Noun Sorting (page 34)

Concrete nouns: apple, apron, barrel, bubble, cloth, dime, hive, jewel, knife, sidewalk

Abstract nouns: anger, honesty, hope, joy, memory, pain, peace, thought, truth, worry

Verb Challenges! (page 35)

1. brought
2. bought
3. chose
4. ate
5. borrowed

More Verb Challenges! (page 36)

Students' word choices will vary.

Past, Present, or Future? (page 37)

1. will cook, future
2. chopped, past
3. shops, present
4. needed, past
5. will bake, future
6. pick, present
7. smells, present
8. added, past
9. mix, present
10. will clean, future or cleaned, past

More Past, Present, or Future? (page 38)

1. opened, past
2. jumped, past
3. will bike, future
4. will bike, future
5. filled, past
6. likes, present
7. will walk, future
8. will walk, future
9. wish, present
10. will borrow, future

Answer Key (cont.)

Be Agreeable! (page 39)

1. are
2. fly
3. collects
4. travel
5. hide
6. capture
7. is
8. lay

Be Agreeable Again! (page 40)

1. his
2. their
3. my
4. it
5. their
6. their
7. their
8. their

Conjunction Junction! (page 41)

1. and
2. but
3. or
4. yet
5. and
6. and; and
7. nor
8. but

Subordinate Conjunctions! (page 42)

1. once
2. after
3. while
4. because
5. so that
6. whenever
7. while
8. whether

Keep It Simple! (page 43)

1. C
2. I
3. I
4. C
5. I
6. C
7. I
8. C
9. I
10. C
11. Students' answers will vary.
12. Students' answers will vary.

Compound It! (page 44)

1. I want to take a walk, and I want to see the sunset.
2. I might watch a movie, or I might play a video game.
3. I walked into town, and I stopped to see my friend.
4. Mom said I could go to town, or Mom said I could stay home.
5. Do you like cats, or do you like dogs?

Complex or Compound? (page 45)

1. ✓ ✓
2. ✓
3. ✓ ✓
4. ✓ ✓
5. ✓
6. ✓ ✓
7. ✓ ✓
8. ✓
9. ✓
10. ✓ ✓

Answer Key (cont.)

Simple, Compound, or Complex? (page 46)

1. S
2. S
3. CC
4. CC
5. C
6. CC
7. CC
8. S
9. CC
10. CC

Movies, Songs, and Plays (page 47)

1. Free Willy
2. The Itsy Bitsy Spider
3. Down by the Station
4. Barney and Friends
5. Home Alone

Books and Capitals! (page 48)

1. The Wonderful Wizard of Oz
2. Twenty Thousand Leagues Under the Sea
3. The Secret Garden
4. Goodnight Moon
5. Pippi Longstocking

Addressing an Envelope (page 49)

Students' answers will vary.

It's Quotable! (page 50)

1. The man said, "You can line up now."
2. Nathan said, "I can't believe we are going on the roller coaster."
3. The woman said, "Fasten your seat belts."
4. Jefferson said, "This is the first time I've ridden a roller coaster."
5. Nathan said, "Wow! This is really fast!"
6. Jefferson screamed, "I think I want off this roller coaster!"
7. Nathan shouted, "Hang on! It's fun!"
8. Jefferson answered, "Whee! I hope this is the last time around!"
9. The woman announced, "Stay seated until the ride stops."
10. Jefferson asked, "Can we do it again?"

In Need of Quotes! (page 51)

1. Students' answers will vary.
2. Students' answers will vary.
3. Students' answers will vary.
4. Students' answers will vary.

Who Owns That? (page 52)

1. the farmer's plow
2. the cow's stall
3. the horse's saddle
4. the chicken's roost
5. the calf's tail
6. the horse's stable
7. the wagon's wheel
8. the garden's plants

Answer Key (cont.)

Plural or Possession? (page 53)
1. dinosaur's
2. dinosaurs
3. museum's
4. scientists
5. adult's
6. body's
7. scientist's
8. years
9. plants; leaves; ferns; mosses
10. animal's; eggs

Meet the OO Families (page 54)

ool family: cool, fool, pool, stool, tool

oon family: croon, goon, loon, moon, noon, soon, spoon

oof family: goof, proof, spoof

Meet Some Letter Patterns (page 55)
1. bowl
2. house
3. brush
4. peas
5. glue
6. train

Take Position! (page 56)
1. ball
2. bell
3. band
4. chair
5. lunch
6. seal

Take Note of K! (page 57)
1. shark
2. sink
3. clock
4. sock
5. lock
6. rock

Syllable Ending Rules (page 58)
1. puzzle
2. apple
3. ankle
4. turtle
5. candle
6. whale

More Syllable Ending Rules (page 59)
1. coordination
2. collection
3. communication
4. construction
5. correction
6. creation
7. decoration
8. direction
9. education
10. election
11. inspection
12. instruction

Hinky Pinky Fun! (page 60)
1. toaster boaster
2. cellar dweller
3. colder folder
4. hopper stopper
5. gory story
6. super snooper
7. fickle pickle
8. witty city

Parts Count! (page 61)
1. aquatics
2. location
3. optimal
4. structure
5. multiple
6. transportation
7. conducts
8. interruption

Answer Key *(cont.)*

Find and Spell (page 62)

1. tongs
2. toothpick
3. tongue
4. tonnage
5. tonsils
6. topknot
7. topsy-turvy
8. toolshed

What Word? (page 63)

1. Students' answers will vary.
2. Students' answers will vary.
3. Students' answers will vary.
4. Students' answers will vary.
5. Students' answers will vary.
6. Students' answers will vary.

Choosing Words (page 64)

1. Students' answers will vary.
2. Students' answers will vary.
3. Students' answers will vary.
4. Students' answers will vary.
5. Students' answers will vary.
6. Students' answers will vary.
7. Students' answers will vary.
8. Students' answers will vary.
9. Students' answers will vary.
10. Students' answers will vary.
11. Students' answers will vary.
12. Students' answers will vary.

Get a Clue! (page 65)

1. I've been feeling sad today.
2. That costs 100 dollars.
3. Go away!
4. I'll hope for you.
5. I need to memorize it.
6. Be patient!

Informal and Formal English (page 66)

1. no
2. romantic
3. when everything goes wrong
4. easily done
5. go away
6. yes
7. between gigantic and enormous
8. tease
9. lose your temper
10. anything you can't recall the name of

The White Mouse (pages 67–68)

1. b
2. a
3. b
4. c
5. a

Achoooo! (pages 69–70)

1. b
2. c
3. c
4. c
5. c

Get to High Ground! (pages 71–72)

1. a
2. c
3. c
4. a
5. b

Up You Go! (pages 73–74)

1. a
2. c
3. b
4. a
5. b

Answer Key (cont.)

Dusty Storms (pages 75–76)
1. b
2. c
3. a
4. c
5. a

NASA at Work (pages 77–78)
1. c
2. a
3. b
4. a
5. b

Power Up with a Nap! (pages 79–80)
1. c
2. a
3. b
4. a
5. c

Sleep Tight! (pages 81–82)
1. b
2. a
3. c
4. a
5. b

The Great American Desert (page 83)
1. investigate
2. groups of people
3. bison
4. empty
5. live
6. dry region

Gold Fever (page 84)
1. gear, tools
2. rough
3. place
4. blanket
5. supplies
6. high, vertical

The American Eagle (page 85)
1. representation
2. length from tip to tip
3. partner
4. baby eagles
5. countrywide
6. guard

A Great Lady (page 86)
1. settlers, newcomers
2. eagerly
3. trip
4. wooden boxes
5. put together
6. stand for

Sidebar Skills (page 87)
1. height, length, length of jaw, length of arms
2. the *Triceratops Horridus'* diet

More Sidebar Skills (page 88)
1. constellations help us navigate around the sky
2. the formation of Ursa Major

Diagram Smarts (page 89)
1. the seasons of Earth
2. Earth tilts around the sun

More Diagrams (page 90)
1. water usage in terms of gallons
2. how to save water

Answer Key (cont.)

The Only Place to Live (page 91)

1. He or she thinks that living by the ocean is the best place to live.
2. He or she thinks that living by the ocean is terrible.

The Best Pet (page 92)

1. He or she thinks that the bull snake is the best pet.
2. He or she thinks that the bull snake makes a bad pet.

Junk Food in Schools (page 93)

1. He or she thinks that junk food is something that should not be found in schools.
2. He or she thinks that junk food should be allowed in schools.

Chores (page 94)

1. He or she thinks that kids should not get paid for doing chores.
2. He or she thinks that kids should get paid for doing chores.

Can You Hear It? (page 95)

1. sound waves
2. vibrates
3. the eardrum
4. make the fluid move and the hair cells bend
5. takes the massage to the brain

Can You Smell It? (page 96)

1. The cilia are tiny hairs that help move mucus out of the lungs.
2. The nose hairs protect the body from initial germs entering the body and the cilia help move the mucus out of the lungs.
3. The olfactory bulb is responsible for identifying scents.

Clean Streets! (page 97)

1. The streets were dirty.
2. He got people to pay for street sweeping and he wrote about the benefits of regular sweeping.
3. The streets were cleaner, people wanted the streets cleaner, and a tax was passed to clean the streets.

Ping… Ping… Ping (page 98)

1. There was no way of finding things in the ocean.
2. He sent out a chirp and measured how long it took for the echo to return.
3. SONAR was invented.

Ka-Boom! (page 99)

1. as toys
2. as weapons
3. He changed them so that they could travel farther.
4. Sir Francis Scott Key saw the rockets and wrote "The Star Spangled Banner."

A Hard-to-Hear Heartbeat (page 100)

1. He remembered that you could put your ear on a piece of wood and hear a pin scratching at the other end.
2. He thought he might be able to hear sound from inside the chest in the same way.
3. He rolled up some paper and made a funnel.
4. He could hear the woman's heart beat.

A Coral Reef (page 101)

1. b
2. a
3. a

Glaciers! (page 102)

1. c
2. a
3. c

Answer Key *(cont.)*

Meaning Match (page 103)
1. bold, daring
2. troublesome
3. round
4. not stopping
5. protector
6. admirable
7. in plain sight
8. most likely
9. feeling
10. odd

More Meaning Match (page 104)
1. message
2. fearfulness
3. hopeful
4. ruling
5. control
6. sensible
7. shortage
8. sharpness
9. kindness
10. honest

Root Detection (page 105)
1. b
2. c
3. c
4. a
5. a
6. a

More Root Detection (page 106)
1. c
2. a
3. c
4. a
5. b
6. b

Dictionaries Rule! (page 107)
1. envious
2. environment
3. enunciation
4. epitaph
5. epidermis
6. envoy
7. epidemic

Glossaries Guide! (page 108)
1. electromagnet
2. phonograph
3. radio waves
4. receiver
5. radio broadcast
6. generator

Literal Meanings (page 109)
1. He is angry and upset.
2. Let's eat.
3. She is in a hurry.
4. It's time for bed.
5. I know how to do it.

More Literal Meanings (page 110)
1. He adored the girl.
2. Be patient.
3. You're blaming the wrong person.
4. You're not the only one.
5. Let's eat a lot.

Word Connections (page 111)

chef's list: appetizer, bake, boil, broil, cook, course, fruit, fry, herb, recipe, spice

teacher's list: assignment, classroom, course, dropout, grade, homework, instruction, principal, school, subject

doctor's list: allergies, bacteria, bandage, checkup, cough, disease, first aid, medicine, painkillers, wound

Answer Key (cont.)

More Word Connections (page 112)

Students' answers will vary.

Meaning Match! (page 113)

1. brave
2. reckless
3. grateful
4. fascinating
5. shy
6. timeless
7. effective
8. dangerous
9. abrupt
10. delicate
11. glum
12. persistent

More Meaning Match! (page 114)

1. suitcases
2. wealth
3. thief
4. hermit
5. cottage
6. celebration
7. diner
8. base
9. rubbish
10. pure
11. refuge
12. peak

It's About Time! (page 115)

1. rarely
2. soon
3. late
4. early
5. always
6. after
7. never
8. usually
9. before
10. later

It's About Position! (page 116)

1. Most people travel by driving <u>in</u> their cars.
2. But some people travel <u>under</u> the ground.
3. Those people often have to walk <u>down</u> the stairs.
4. Then they get <u>on</u> a platform.
5. When the subway arrives, they have to get <u>inside</u> the car quickly.
6. When they arrive <u>at</u> the station, they get out <u>of</u> the subway.
7. They probably have to go <u>up</u> the stairs or escalator.
8. They may have to walk <u>along</u> a hallway to catch another subway.
9. The first subway was built <u>in</u> London.
10. Take a subway the next time you go <u>to</u> a big city. It's fun!

Clang! Clang! (page 117)

1. b
2. slippery streets, steep hills, heavy loads
3. Students' answers will vary.

Earthquake! (page 118)

1. b
2. your bed might sway back and forth, books might fall off your shelf
3. Students' answers will vary.

Answer Key (cont.)

Dangerous Waves! (page 119)

1. a sudden disruption of the sea's surface, an earthquake, a volcano that explodes
2. an earthquake
3. it destroyed many buildings and thousands of people were killed

The Olympics (page 120)

1. they are held every four years, they took a lot of preparation, they had music, they had special displays
2. there was only one race, they wrestled and threw spears, they raced chariots
3. The pankration is a game where contestants fight until they give up or die.

Fables (page 121)

1. He broke up the fight between the eagle and the snake.
2. He prevented the man from drinking the poisoned water.
3. a

Fable Message (page 122)

1. He wished to change himself.
2. c

Another Fable Message (page 123)

1. The town mouse liked living on the edge and the country mouse was more simple.
2. b

More Fables (page 124)

1. She told the wolf that she would not come down lower so that he could eat her.
2. a

What Does It Really Mean? (page 125)

1. It's better to have something that is certain than taking a risk for more.
2. You can't change who you are.
3. They are easy to get or inexpensive.
4. They are very expensive.
5. Even tough times have something good about them.
6. Don't go where you shouldn't.
7. They are willing to help.
8. Time to be serious,

More Sayings to Learn (page 126)

1. It's worth saving everything you can.
2. Don't limit your options.
3. Don't talk.
4. Don't make things worse.
5. Don't rely on something unknown.
6. Everyone is dealing with the same problem.
7. It's definitely going to happen.
8. Take a risk.

The Written Word (page 127)

1. play
2. script
3. act
4. scene
5. chapter
6. stanza
7. glossary; index

Mood Match (page 128)

1. playfulness
2. loneliness
3. joy
4. anger
5. kindness
6. fear

Comparison Chart (page 129)

Students' answers will vary.

Answer Key (cont.)

Compare Characters (page 130)

Students' answers will vary.

A Real Hero (page 133)

Students' answers will vary.

Can You Explain That? (page 134)

Students' answers will vary.

Cause and Effect (page 135)

Students' answers will vary.

Have a Great Trip! (page 136)

Students' answers will vary.

Research (pages 139–140)

Students' answers will vary.

Number Round-Up! (page 144)

1.	30	11.	70
2.	70	12.	10
3.	40	13.	50
4.	40	14.	20
5.	80	15.	10
6.	60	16.	90
7.	80	17.	20
8.	10	18.	20
9.	20	19.	90
10.	30	20.	50

More Tens Round-Up (page 145)

1.	50	11.	70
2.	80	12.	90
3.	30	13.	50
4.	70	14.	30
5.	90	15.	20
6.	90	16.	70
7.	70	17.	10
8.	20	18.	20
9.	20	19.	50
10.	10	20.	60

Big Number Round-Up! (page 146)

1.	130	11.	680
2.	170	12.	430
3.	810	13.	680
4.	170	14.	730
5.	510	15.	260
6.	390	16.	190
7.	230	17.	260
8.	100	18.	910
9.	440	19.	100
10.	990	20.	350

More Big Number Round-Up! (page 147)

1.	420	11.	760
2.	240	12.	470
3.	870	13.	990
4.	720	14.	190
5.	190	15.	100
6.	700	16.	190
7.	500	17.	240
8.	920	18.	710
9.	140	19.	230
10.	560	20.	570

Add Big Numbers! (page 148)

1. 200 + 50 + 4; 700 + 20 + 7; 981 = 900 + 70 + 11
2. 300 + 60 + 9; 500 + 10 + 4; 883 = 800 + 70 + 13
3. 500 + 50 + 5; 200 + 10 + 7; 772 = 700 + 60 + 12
4. 100 + 70 + 4; 800 + 40 + 3; 1,017 = 900 + 110 + 7
5. 100 + 60 + 2; 800 + 50 + 2; 1,014 = 900 + 110 + 4
6. 200 + 30 + 4; 100 + 50 + 6; 390 = 300 + 80 + 10

Answer Key (cont.)

Add More Big Numbers (page 149)

1. 925
2. 592
3. 781
4. 288
5. 732
6. 890
7. 990
8. 998

Add Even More Big Numbers! (page 150)

1. 522
2. 650
3. 268
4. 902
5. 932
6. 210
7. 478
8. 910
9. 910

Subtract Big Numbers! (page 151)

1. 700 + 20 + 7; 200 + 10 + 4;
   513 = 500 + 10 + 3
2. 500 + 90 + 8; 500 + 10 + 4;
   84 = 80 + 4
3. 400 + 40 + 8; 200 + 10 + 7;
   231 = 200 + 30 + 1
4. 400 + 70 + 4; 200 + 40 + 1;
   233 = 200 + 30 + 3
5. 900 + 60 + 2; 700 + 50 + 2;
   210 = 200 + 10 + 0
6. 900 + 90 + 9; 700 + 50 + 6;
   243 = 200 + 40 + 3
7. 800 + 80; 100 + 60; 720 = 700 + 20
8. 600 + 60 + 6; 300 + 30 + 3;
   333 = 300 + 30 + 3

Subtract More Big Numbers! (page 152)

1. 237
2. 445
3. 109
4. 218
5. 728
6. 158

Subtract Even More Big Numbers! (page 153)

1. 386
2. 89
3. 269
4. 95
5. 99
6. 9
7. 184
8. 89
9. 270

It's All About Tens! (page 154)

1. 10 dots
2. 20 dots
3. 30 dots
4. 40 dots
5. 50 dots
6. 60 dots
7. 70 dots
8. 80 dots
9. 90 dots
10. 100 dots

Multiply Those Tens! (page 155)

1. 20
2. 60
3. 70
4. 10
5. 10
6. 40
7. 40
8. 20
9. 30
10. 30
11. 60
12. 50
13. 80
14. 80
15. 50
16. 70
17. 90
18. 90
19. 100
20. 0

Multiply More Tens! (page 156)

1. 10
2. 7
3. 4
4. 6
5. 1
6. 8
7. 5
8. 9
9. 3
10. 0
11. 4
12. 6
13. 8
14. 9
15. 0
16. 7
17. 2
18. 1
19. 5
20. 3

Find the Number! (page 157)

1. 24
2. 16
3. 8
4. 20
5. 4
6. 32
7. 12
8. 28
9. 16
10. 12
11. 36
12. 20

Answer Key (cont.)

Find More Numbers! (page 158)
1. 27
2. 12
3. 24
4. 6
5. 15
6. 3
7. 18
8. 30
9. 27
10. 9
11. 21
12. 3

Sticky Groups! (page 160)
1. 10
2. 50
3. 6
4. 20
5. 25

More Sticky Groups! (page 161)
1. 10
2. 5
3. 14; 21
4. 28; 35
5. 35; 42
6. 56; 63

Money Problems (page 162)
1. $20.00
2. $20.00
3. $20.00
4. $25.00; $5 \times 5 = 25$
5. $15.00; $10.00

Got Milk? (page 163)
1. 10 gallons; $1 \times 10 = 10$
2. 8 gallons; $2 \times 4 = 8$
3. $10.00
4. 9 gallons; $3 \times 3 = 9$

Missing Multipliers (page 164)
1. 5
2. 10
3. 6
4. 3
5. 8
6. 4
7. 6
8. 9
9. 6
10. 7
11. 9
12. 9
13. 4
14. 8
15. 4
16. 9
17. 8
18. 5

More Missing Multipliers (page 165)
1. 8
2. 10
3. 10
4. 9
5. 9
6. 2
7. 5
8. 11
9. 9
10. 9
11. 8
12. 2
13. 5
14. 5
15. 8
16. 7
17. 10
18. 1

Missing Numbers (page 166)
1. 2
2. 3
3. 14
4. 9
5. 34
6. 12
7. 11
8. 6
9. 4
10. 2
11. 15
12. 9
13. 7
14. 6
15. 4
16. 14
17. 10
18. 4

Multiply Either Way (page 167)
1. 2; 16; 16
2. 1; 6; 6
3. 2; 14; 14
4. 3; 12; 12
5. 4; 8; 8
6. 0; 0; 0
7. 7; 56; 56
8. 3; 15; 15
9. 2; 22; 22
10. 6; 24; 24
11. 1; 9; 9
12. 6; 30; 30

Associative Property of Multiplication at Work (page 168)
1. 12; 36
2. 22; 44
3. 3; 27
4. 6; 24
5. 4; 28
6. 21; 105
7. 40; 240
8. 30; 210

Answer Key *(cont.)*

Multiply in Steps! (page 169)
1. 8; 72
2. 9; 36
3. 80; 240
4. 6; 42
5. 11; 55
6. 60; 120
7. 20; 160
8. 10; 90

Choose the Steps! (page 170)
1. 6; 4; 24
2. 24; 1; 24
3. 12; 5; 60
4. 10; 3; 30
5. 80; 2; 160
6. 48; 1; 48
7. 20; 1; 20
8. 12; 9; 108

Divide Up the Sticks! (page 171)
1. 8; 8
2. 5; 5
3. 2; 2
4. 9; 9

Multiply and Divide Them Up! (page 172)
1. 9; 9
2. 25; 25
3. 7; 7
4. 12; 12
5. 4; 4
6. 10; 10
7. 11; 11
8. 11; 11
9. 6; 6

More Problems to Multiply and Divide (page 173)
1. 11; 11
2. 9; 9
3. 6; 6
4. 6; 6
5. 4; 4
6. 10; 10
7. 11; 11
8. 12; 12
9. 8; 8

Big Problems (page 174)
1. $9 \times 4 = 36$; $9 \times 3 = 27$;
   $36 + 27 = 63$; $63.00
2. $14,014 + 14,270 = 28,284$;
   $40,000 - 28,284 = 11,716$;
   11,716 feet

More Big Problems! (page 175)
1. $6 \times 5 = 30$; $2 \times 3 = 6$;
   $30 + 6 = 36$; $86 - 36 = 50$;
   50 spaces
2. $11 \times 4 = 44$; $6 \times 4 = 24$;
   $44 + 24 = 68$; $68 - 60 = 8$;
   $8

Fraction Fun! (page 176)
1. $\frac{2}{3}$
2. $\frac{1}{4}$
3. $\frac{2}{4}$
4. $\frac{1}{3}$
5. $\frac{3}{10}$
6. $\frac{5}{16}$

More Fraction Fun! (page 177)
1.
2.
3.
4.
5.
6.

Fractions on a Line (page 178)
1. 4
2. 1
3. $\frac{1}{4}$

Line Up for Fractions! (page 179)
1. $0; \frac{1}{4}; \frac{2}{4}; \frac{3}{4}; 1$
2. $0; \frac{1}{5}; \frac{2}{5}; \frac{3}{5}; \frac{4}{5}; \frac{5}{5}$
3. $0; \frac{1}{3}; \frac{2}{3}; \frac{3}{3}$
4. $0; \frac{1}{6}; \frac{2}{6}; \frac{3}{6}; \frac{4}{6}; \frac{5}{6}; \frac{6}{6}$

#50886—Bright & Brainy: 3rd Grade Practice

Answer Key (cont.)

Find Equal Fractions (page 180)

1. 1
2. 2
3. 4
4. 8
5. 16
6. $\frac{4}{8}$; $\frac{8}{16}$

Find Equal and Unequal Fractions (page 181)

1. $\frac{3}{6}$; $\frac{4}{8}$; $\frac{5}{10}$
2. $\frac{2}{6}$; $\frac{3}{9}$
3. $\frac{4}{10}$
4. $\frac{3}{8}$; $\frac{5}{8}$

Make a Fraction Chart (page 182)

1									
$\frac{1}{2}$					$\frac{1}{2}$				
$\frac{1}{3}$			$\frac{1}{3}$			$\frac{1}{3}$			
$\frac{1}{4}$		$\frac{1}{4}$		$\frac{1}{4}$			$\frac{1}{4}$		
$\frac{1}{5}$		$\frac{1}{5}$		$\frac{1}{5}$		$\frac{1}{5}$		$\frac{1}{5}$	
$\frac{1}{6}$		$\frac{1}{6}$	$\frac{1}{6}$		$\frac{1}{6}$		$\frac{1}{6}$		$\frac{1}{6}$
$\frac{1}{7}$	$\frac{1}{7}$	$\frac{1}{7}$	$\frac{1}{7}$	$\frac{1}{7}$	$\frac{1}{7}$		$\frac{1}{7}$		
$\frac{1}{8}$	$\frac{1}{8}$	$\frac{1}{8}$	$\frac{1}{8}$	$\frac{1}{8}$	$\frac{1}{8}$	$\frac{1}{8}$	$\frac{1}{8}$		
$\frac{1}{9}$	$\frac{1}{9}$	$\frac{1}{9}$	$\frac{1}{9}$	$\frac{1}{9}$	$\frac{1}{9}$	$\frac{1}{9}$	$\frac{1}{9}$	$\frac{1}{9}$	
$\frac{1}{10}$	$\frac{1}{10}$	$\frac{1}{10}$	$\frac{1}{10}$	$\frac{1}{10}$	$\frac{1}{10}$	$\frac{1}{10}$	$\frac{1}{10}$	$\frac{1}{10}$	$\frac{1}{10}$

Find the Fractions (page 183)

1. $\frac{1}{2}$; $\frac{2}{4}$; $\frac{3}{6}$; $\frac{4}{8}$
2. $\frac{3}{5}$
3. $\frac{1}{3}$; $\frac{2}{6}$
4. $\frac{1}{4}$
5. $\frac{1}{1}$; $\frac{2}{2}$; $\frac{3}{3}$; $\frac{4}{4}$; $\frac{5}{5}$; $\frac{6}{6}$; $\frac{8}{8}$; $\frac{9}{9}$; $\frac{10}{10}$
6. $\frac{1}{3}$; $\frac{3}{9}$
7. $\frac{4}{10}$
8. $\frac{2}{8}$
9. $\frac{4}{6}$; $\frac{6}{9}$
10. $\frac{2}{4}$; $\frac{3}{6}$; $\frac{4}{8}$; $\frac{5}{10}$

The Whole Thing (page 184)

1. $\frac{1}{1} + \frac{1}{1} + \frac{1}{1} = \frac{3}{1}$; 3
2. $\frac{1}{1} + \frac{1}{1} + \frac{1}{1} + \frac{1}{1} + \frac{1}{1} = \frac{5}{1}$; 5
3. $\frac{1}{1} + \frac{1}{1} + \frac{1}{1} + \frac{1}{1} + \frac{1}{1} + \frac{1}{1} + \frac{1}{1} + \frac{1}{1} = \frac{8}{1}$; 8

Mix It Up! (page 185)

1. whole; 3
2. mixed; $2\frac{1}{2}$
3. mixed; $3\frac{1}{2}$
4. whole; 1
5. mixed; $4\frac{1}{2}$

What's the Size? (page 186)

1. $\frac{1}{8} < \frac{1}{4}$
2. $\frac{1}{3} > \frac{1}{6}$
3. $\frac{5}{6} > \frac{1}{3}$
4. $\frac{4}{8} = \frac{1}{2}$

Compare Sizes (page 187)

1. $\frac{3}{8}$; $\frac{1}{4}$; $\frac{3}{8} > \frac{1}{4}$
2. $\frac{5}{6}$; $\frac{7}{8}$; $\frac{5}{6} < \frac{7}{8}$
3. $\frac{1}{3}$; $\frac{1}{2}$; $\frac{1}{3} < \frac{1}{2}$
4. $\frac{4}{7}$; $\frac{4}{8}$; $\frac{4}{7} > \frac{4}{8}$

Compare Sizes of Fractions (page 188)

1. $\frac{1}{2} > \frac{3}{8}$
2. ; $\frac{3}{6} = \frac{1}{2}$
3. ; $\frac{3}{4} > \frac{5}{8}$
4. ; $\frac{1}{3} < \frac{1}{2}$

Tell Time (page 189)

1. 7:30 A.M.; 7:10 A.M.; 7:30 A.M.
2. 1:30 P.M.; 9:00 A.M.; 1:30 P.M.
3. 2:00 P.M.; 11:45 A.M.; 2:00 P.M.
4. 6:30 P.M.; 6:30 P.M.; 10:00 P.M.

Answer Key (cont.)

How Much Time? (page 190)
1. 50 minutes; 6:20 A.M.; 7:10 A.M.
2. 7; 15; 8:30 A.M.; 3:45 P.M.
3. 3; 30; 8:15 A.M.; 11:45 A.M.
4. 1; 15; 7:45 P.M.; 9:00 P.M.

Measure Liters (page 191)
1. a
2. a
3. c
4. a
5. b

Weighing Grams and Kilograms (page 192)
1. g
2. g
3. kg
4. g
5. kg
6. kg
7. g
8. g
9. kg
10. g

Graph those Worms! (page 193)
1. 17
2. 40
3. Dad and Zenia
4. 22
5. 57

Bar Graph (page 194)
1. 30
2. 20
3. Health
4. Math and Science
5. 100

Create Your Own Bar Graph (page 195)
1. Students' answers will vary.
2. Students' answers will vary.
3. Students' answers will vary.
4. Students' answers will vary.
5. Students' answers will vary.

Measure Up! (page 196)
1. Students' answers will vary.
2. Students' answers will vary.
3. Students' answers will vary.
4. Students' answers will vary.
5. Students' answers will vary.
6. Students' answers will vary.
7. Students' answers will vary.
8. Students' answers will vary.
9. Students' answers will vary.
10. Students' answers will vary.

Measure by the Foot! (page 197)
1. Students' answers will vary.
2. Students' answers will vary.
3. Students' answers will vary.
4. Students' answers will vary.
5. Students' answers will vary.
6. Students' answers will vary.
7. Students' answers will vary.
8. Students' answers will vary.
9. Students' answers will vary.
10. Students' answers will vary.

What About Area? (page 198)
1. 8
2. 12
3. 12
4. 10
5. 24
6. 10
7. 6
8. 20

Answer Key (cont.)

Find the Area (page 199)

1. 9
2. 7
3. 20
4. 8
5. 9
6. 24

The Area Formula (page 200)

1. 4; 3; 4; 3; 12
2. 6; 2; 6; 2; 12
3. 6; 4; 6; 4; 24
4. 10; 1; 10; 1; 10

Measure the Area (page 201)

1. Students' answers will vary.
2. Students' answers will vary.
3. Students' answers will vary.
4. Students' answers will vary.

Measure More Areas (page 202)

1. Students' answers will vary.
2. Students' answers will vary.
3. Students' answers will vary.
4. Students' answers will vary.

Problem Areas! (page 203)

1. $20 \times 12 = 240$ square feet;
   $240 \div 2 = 120$ square feet
2. $9 \times 12 = 108$ square feet;
   $108 \div 2 = 54$ square feet;
   $4 \times 8 = 32$ square feet;
   22 square feet

More Problem Areas! (page 204)

1. $10 \times 13 = 130$ square feet;
   $11 \times 12 = 132$ square feet;
   Bedroom 2; 2 square feet
2. $2 \times 5 = 10$ square feet;
   $2 \times 6 = 12$ square feet;
   $2 \times 3 = 6$ square feet;
   $2 \times 3 = 6$ square feet;
   34 square feet of granite;
   $10 \times 6 = 60$ square feet
   yes

Still More Problem Areas! (page 205)

1. $96 \div 6 = 16$ panels;
   $6 \times 8 = 48$ square feet;
   $48 \times 16 = 768$ square feet
2. $12 \times 15 = 180$ square feet;
   $11 \times 13 = 143$ square feet;
   $14 \times 15 = 210$ square feet;
   $8 \times 7 = 56$ square feet;
   589 square feet

Computing Irregular Areas (page 206)

1. Section A: $1 \times 1 = 1$ square foot;
   Section B: $4 \times 2 = 8$ square feet;
   $1 + 8 = 9$ square feet
2. Section A: $2 \times 5 = 10$ square feet;
   Section B: $1 \times 5 = 5$ square feet;
   $10 + 5 = 15$ square feet

More Irregular Area Computations (page 207)

1. Section A: $3 \times 3 = 9$ square feet;
   Section B: $2 \times 3 = 6$ square feet;
   $9 + 6 = 15$ square feet
2. Section A: $3 \times 4 = 12$ square feet;
   Section B: $2 \times 3 = 6$ square feet;
   Section C: $1 \times 2 = 2$ square feet;
   $12 + 6 + 2 = 20$ square feet

Answer Key (cont.)

Perimeter (page 208)

    1. 14

    2. 24

    3. 22

    4. 18

More Perimeters (page 209)

    1. 24

    2. 26

    3. 18

    4. 20

Some More Perimeters (page 210)

    1. 20

    2. 22

    3. 18

    4. 18

Identify Polygons (page 211)

Students should outline the polygons.

Identify Quadrilaterals (page 212)

Students should outline the quadrilaterals.

Find Shapes (page 213)

Students' answers will vary.

Divide These Shapes (page 214)

Students' answers will vary. The following are some suggestions:

    1.

    2.

    3.

    4.

    5.

Contents of the Resource CD

Contents of the Resource CD (cont.)

Contents of the Resource CD (cont.)

Notes